Hearsay from Heaven and Hades

New Orleans Secrets of Sinners and Saints

Hearsay from Heaven and Hades

New Orleans Secrets of Sinners and Saints

TJ Fisher

Illustrations by Jennifer Porter

MORGANA
PRESS

First edition

ISBN-13: 978-0-9773514-3-5

Library of Congress Control Number: 2007937443

10 9 8 7 6 5 4 3 2 1

Front cover design: Jedd Haas and Skip Bolen

Back cover and book design: Jedd Haas

Editor: Ron Kenner

Printed in China by Imago

Published by Morgana Press
822 Chartres Street
New Orleans, LA 70116
Visit our website at www.morganapress.com

Acknowledgment

A special acknowledgment and tribute goes to my most special friend, one who has moved and touched me deeply — an incredible woman of the type of unsurpassable faith, fortitude, strength, grace and dignity that most of us can only dream about; a beautiful woman of eight decades who still smiles, walks to work, consoles others and leads joyous second-line parades, all in the shadow of unfathomable heartache and loss. This is the esteemed and beloved Miss Marion Colbert of Treme, the real face, heart and soul of the Great American City of New Orleans.

And respects to the historic St. Augustine Catholic Church of New Orleans, Miss Marion's parish (and home of the legendary Jazz Mass), the oldest African-American parish in the United States (a canonically established parish since 1842); thank you for accepting and blessing those of us who do not always walk in Miss Marion's forever kind, and righteous, and loving and forgiving path. May the powers-that-be in Rome and elsewhere see the light and significance in keeping this remarkable spirit-filled treasure alive; with respect to continuing to fund the survival of this most unique parish which so well represents the people, places and culture of New Orleans. St. Augustine, home of the "Tomb of the Unknown Slave," of the shackles borne by bygone years and of Congo Square, is a living piece of history, a storied place of blood, sweat and tears, of hope, survival and more.

Miss Marion's parish is the longtime symbolic yet still-struggling beating heart, rhythm and soul of one of our oldest cities, a cultural treasure and icon, an egalitarian taproot of diversity, a place that ought not sink and pass away in our nation's memory.

St. Augustine, located in the Treme neighborhood of New Orleans, advocates and celebrates freedom from "sin and oppression," welcoming sinners and saints alike through its age-old doors. Since its dedication in 1842, St. Augustine (a property with its proud history dating back to 1720), has been a church and a congregation of people of all colors, originally inviting both free people and slaves as worshippers. It continues on as a beacon of humanity and spirituality to all, both as a history lesson of America and a shining example of twenty-first century Christianity in action. A true New Orleans-style sanctuary remains dedicated to and accepting of all, both the fallen and the ascended; regardless of personal beliefs, convictions or denominations, visitors and members are invited to enter, and to feel what New Orleanians feel.

Dedication

My work is dedicated to the memory and the stories of the
people and the history of New Orleans — past, present and
future — in particular to the beloved families, friends, pets,
homes and dreams ravished and forever lost to Katrina, as well as
to that which has survived reborn; to the celebration of triumph
over sorrow, the defeat of dark days; and to my soul-mate, the one
whom I loved long before I ever knew him and who rescued me
from peril. Although we shall miss what is gone and is no more,
the unyielding fingerprints of time that lie heavy upon our hearts,
we hold fast to what we have left, in the here and now. Our laughter
shall overcome our tears. New Orleans remains a city of magical
thinking, looking to upright, reclaim and recover the broken
parts of itself upon the wings of hope. We believe in tomorrow,
yesterday and today; may our faith and fate collide and dovetail as
one. We shall remember always. Beauty here is born of three
hundred years of wisdom and experience, collapse and revival,
laughter and grief. No matter how unforgiving the wilderness, or
deep the well of darkness, New Orleanians, like those who came
before, now persevere and look for the eternal light, rebirth and
renaissance of the city we love.

Beyond the Watermark

—◆—

40 Days, 40 Nights

—◆—

Down in New Orleans

Contents

POSTSCRIPT: OUR DEFINING MOMENT

AUTHOR LAGNIAPPE

Prelusion from Rue Bourbon

I am TJ Fisher and I live on Bourbon Street in New
Orleans, a town like none other, a magical place filled with
whimsical and firebrand people who relish a "never-a-dull-
moment" sense of daring and commitment. We French
Quarterites are long recognized as impetuous, idealistic
romanticists with a curious proclivity for surreal drama. You
could say we are unafraid of lending fodder for gossip. Here
the time-honored circle of rosary beads, revelry and rue come
together. We engage in famously public feuds and vocal
challenges. A colorful citizenry, we share a sharp sense of
humor and a flamboyant nature. Intriguing tales of our
unconventionalities abound. And post-Katrina, we are more
outspoken than ever.

A wildly personal place, our customs, sacraments and
superstitions do not fit easily into any one category. That is
what makes us particularly interesting, entertaining, amusing
and controversial. We are a community of rich ethnicities,
religions, opinions. Our ancient city is a unique place of
worship and frolic, introspection and self-discovery — for the
holy and hedonistic alike. We are mainly spiritual and yet

separate and aloof, sometimes religious and sometimes not, as we are deeply influenced by our existence and death on the edge. Known to be unorthodox, ideological, cryptic and philosophical, we often take what we want from Catholicism, Baptism, Judaism and Voodooism — forming new conjunctions with our own cherished traditions. The truth is that we take in life with a different set of eyes, with an open and caring "anything-goes" attitude. *Le Bon Temps Roule*. Some call us idiosyncratic and iconoclastic, and it is true. Passions run rampant. Emotions are poured, provoked and stirred. Senses ignited. The spirit and soul of our city — our unique history, culture and customs — reign supreme.

New Orleanians understand the intrigue and inspiration of traipsing beyond life's detours and dreams deferred. Life here is fraught with extraordinary troubles, struggles, conflicts and complications; yet that which we grapple with and enshrine causes us to flourish as we climb and descend the up-down winding spirals of destiny. Illusions shatter but we continue to find deep reflections, inspiration and solace in the ring of memories captured in the shade of ancestors and in what the past has taught us. Yes, Louisianians court danger and controversy without a second thought. Especially the illogical, the complicated, the impossible and the soulful appeal to us. We value listening to the heart over the head, trusting in spontaneity and risk over calculation; we believe in the power of instinct over reason, in forgiveness over judgment, in impermanence over permanence, in tradition over the trendy. We believe in these things but are not brainless and, highly alert to the substance of things, are often astute; not least with the benefit of painfully sharp perceptions.

Those who choose to live and visit here on the edge of timelessness find the draw, allure and exotic personality of New Orleans irresistible and inexplicable; our characters are presumed eccentric and quaint, outlandish and secretive, yet keenly intimate and warm. This is a consuming and compelling place that charms, captivates, galvanizes and unleashes people in equal measure. New Orleans is our muse, our love, our heart, our spirit, our joy, and our sorrow. We are wedded to her and to her mists of time, to the continuation of the past in the present. New Orleans is a place of reoccurring themes, enfolded and new again. Here history and timeworn images are treasured, not feared. That as well as echoes. I believe there are truths in truisms. Evocative. Old stories remain, remembered and relived.

New Orleanians do not follow trends or do things "by the book." We are immune to what is passé. You do not have to be a seer or a sage to see that in an increasingly bland world where many endlessly seek novelty and newness, people will always find comfort in and connection with familiarity, repetition, customs, heritage, ritual and things that reek of old age, patina and soul. The roots and threads of cliché take hold and twist into something original.

The attributes that the national media often uses to malign New Orleans are in fact true. Depending on where you stand, our city is immersed in ethos, mythos and pathos, truth and lies. Yet all can be portrayed in a gripping or malicious way. Enigmatic and veiled or stark and dark. Pre-Katrina we were regaled for the distinctive qualities that set us apart, what made us different, what attracted people; post-Katrina, the naysayers of the world damn us for possessing many of those very same characteristics that previously kept us from being Anywhere-USA. Yes, we have artists and the card readers in Jackson Square, ghost tours, carriages, second-line parades, street entertainers, formality and debauchery cohabiting; in my block I like seeing a miniature horse, an alligator-size lizard, a guy with a snake draped around his neck, and costumed people rubbing shoulders with those cloaked in black-tie attire (with requisite drinks in hand) as they saunter beneath my balcony. I like *Theatre d'Orléans*. It would not be the same if recreated in suburbia. It is not the same at (the French Quarter of) Disney World or Las Vegas. We love the French Quarter precisely because it is the Quarter, not prissy and perfect. A place where blemishes and imperfections are welcome. Applauded. We rebel against gentrification and homogenization. Frankly, most of us here prefer a little poison in our paradise.

My life and my work revolve around the French Quarter. She has left her indelible imprint on me. Each work is wildly different, yet I see a continuation of the twisty gossamer and braided threads that entangle me. We can never close our eyes to what we have seen and loved. That probably gives some slight clue as to my current state of mind and why I am so hopelessly enmeshed in the paradoxical terrain that is New Orleans.

Locals are free to pursue and investigate the dark fringes, dramas and complexities of the human condition, the mystique and mix of mingling with flawed people. We ricochet between the paradigms of high and low culture, between scandal and sanctity. Our multilayered alluvial sludge makes for a rich and inviting back-story, a siren's song from which to draw creativity, courage and inspiration. This *is* New Orleans, Louisiana, where the people, places, voices, memories, stories and visions are not only memorable but also unforgettable. Come share our cocktail and church chitchat secrets, our obituaries and risings, our gossips and misgivings, and live our life....

What is *Hearsay from Heaven and Hades*?

It is a mischievous work meant for those with a sense of satire, a mocking heart, a deep soul, and a knowledge of what both heaven and hell on earth feel like, up close and personal. If you fear turmoil in real life or consider yourself overly innocent and prim and proper, read no further. These aphorisms have not been cleansed. They are uncensored and contentious, irreverent and satirical, sad and funny; just like the contradictory flow of conscience that flashes though all our heads — things we think but rarely say aloud.

New Orleans is an inescapably epic city that is fragile, beautiful, haunting, tragic and erotic; teeming with life and death, and the ties of memories. Yet beware. The New Orleans lifestyle and our philosophies are not for those who seek to be perpetually stranded in a stunted land of vapid and syrupy crystallized happiness of fake goodie-two-shoes positiveness with no dark edges. Here in Louisiana we dance, dream, scream and cry in the city, down in the swampland, and on the floodplains. Another world unto ourselves, we are allowed to parade our sentiments and convictions on our seersucker sleeves and tattooed arms. We emblazon our comments on our balcony flags that flap in the fragile shadows of the vanishing wetlands and the mighty old Mississippi River. We wear our fears and angers on our faces and we say what we really think about love, loss, lust, betrayal, backstabbing and survival on the brink. There is no other place like New Orleans and there never will be.

Our soil is richer than any character study or scenario of right or wrong, good or bad, politics or peccadilloes. Indeed, mother does not always know best. Beyond our prayers there are curses, and even spells. Sometimes it is okay, even essential, to take off the white kid gloves, to crawl and fight and get mean, lowdown and dirty; to take the dare and the challenge like the "gentleman" duelers of days of old. Seeping like mist from our crumbling walls, hidden deep within our secret gardens, locals and outsiders hear whisperings of embedded dark and enchanted satire, musings and witticisms and rumblings that expose a deep swatch in the psyche. The lifestyle here is one of saints and sinners, of elegance and decadence, all festooned and melded together into an odd collective consciousness. The silt of our convoluted lives is steamy and storied, and once you drink from the fountain that is the Vieux Carré it is impossible to willingly give up the strange communion of camaraderie; it infiltrates the French Quarter, along with the rest of our flood-and-hurricane-prone city.

Indeed, Katrina was the high disaster that seemingly stripped us to the marrow of our bones, forcing us to grapple with runaway misery, anger and sadness, and to this day, and probably forever, torrents of emotional upheaval and words still flow out of us like floodwaters. But we are not the first and will not be the last to see the other side. Nowadays, as in decades and centuries past, we overtop the rules of normal convention and polite society. Our unrestrained thoughts, attitudes, actions and voices cannot be turned back or tamed or silenced. Sometimes we run from — yet rush to and embrace — the hush-hush subject matter that sneakily slips behind the eyes, into the head, underneath the skin. I am speaking of an unusual willingness to go deep, to ask questions and probe the boundaries, emotionally, psychologically, physically and spiritually. The picture is not always rosy, but it is vivid and meaningful; at times enchanting, at other times dank, even horrifying. From the hallowed halls of stylish tycoons to the underbelly of pop-culture and fractured people living in the abyss, from beyond the revelry and merrymaking, the guises and disguises, here in New Orleans lies a quirky shadow dance of quips, dark-jewel slices of life, rapid-fire lessons and rules to live by.

New Orleanians are a pithy people. A flinty bunch. Edgy. Playful. Passionate. Resourceful. Introspective. Poignant. Sweet. Sarcastic. Wicked. Sad. Droll. Funny. Raw. Bracing. Transporting. And so here is to those who refuse allegiance to stone, who seek truth beyond the masquerade and façade. We know that death waits outside the door. Yet we still laugh, parade, celebrate, dance, worship, mock ourselves and others — and throw a party like nobody can. The horrors and nightmares (and, yet, enlightenments and even redemptions) of Katrina, the unspeakable devotions and truths we have seen laid bare, the things we now know, have forced us to unlock ourselves as people, as writers, as storytellers. Those who know what it means to miss New Orleans love to bask in, laugh at and cry for juicy and delectable ruminations; that which raises eyebrows, curls lips, snags heads and will not let go. We give credence to things unseen, and unknown and unproven, as well as to that impossible-to-silence "little voice" that lurks inside all of us.

People willing to walk on the edge of dawn and darkness are drawn to seek out chronicles of contemplative and introspective prose written on water — motley assortments of lingering pulp-truth rhapsodies, riddles, ridicules, treacheries and obsessions. Our own self-deprecating and stylized depictions of French Quarter-style manners and morals include witty inquiries into the "celebration" of a place that straddles the precipice that lies just above and below sea level. New Orleans is, and will always be, a fascinating tableau of time and vicissitudes.

When you live here or visit here, seeing the slant and coloring of our multi-hued streets and alleyways, one cannot help but find an engrossing loaded powder keg of quixotic 24-karat angel-devil dust.

Here you see and unveil images that rise from the humidity and come to life: walking journals and dancing ghosts of the inner thoughts of cinematic characters — of paradoxical proverbs and provocative murmurings, of unscrupulous ideas, mutterings, sayings, ironies, warnings and regrets, of aspects overheard, stated, repeated, dreamed, promised, prophesized, lamented, of words written, rewritten, polished and sharpened over the years. I believe it is impossible to write anything about New Orleans without the fierce emotion and attachment of a lover. She has a soul that lives in the sodden soil that can never be erased or stripped away; it seeps into us, clings to us, and we carry it with us everywhere we go.

Our city is a renaissance of what French Quarterites have embraced for three hundred years — an unvarnished carousel of life at once capricious, cruel, kind, entertaining, murky, dreamlike, dangerous, mysterious, mad, mocking, contradictory, absurd, otherworldly, farcical and allegorical. This sardonic handbook is intended for anyone with a yen to be a saint, sinner, survivor, winner, loser, pathbreaker, tastemaker, rebel, renegade, maverick, rogue, rabble-rouser, nonconformist, malcontent, misfit, visionary, hero, coward, pirate, prophet or philosopher — that is, for those who seek to explore and fan the flames, the ecstasy and agony of the human existence. No prerequisite experience is required to jump down the rabbit hole of Louisiana soil. To get bitten by the Creole and Cajun fever.

You ask, why is the book and "voice" born of the French Quarter? Louisiana, New Orleans and the French Quarter in particular have always been an intriguingly ripe Mecca, an historic convergence point for writers and artistically creative persons of all types. Those who love a colorful life, an existence permeated with jagged-edged wit, barbed black humor, sophistication and wisdom find the "home of their heart" here in New Orleans. For here we are free to openly gallivant through conscious and unconscious feelings, fears and personal knowledge, recapturing an awareness deeply buried yet simmering within the ever unfaithful and sly head, heart, body and soul. Whether born here or transplanted, New Orleanians somehow instinctually understand that the age-old griefs and galas go hand-in-hand. We are perfectly free to tilt off center with socially, politically, morally diverse viewpoints. We clash, but we get along. New Orleans has always eagerly espoused a slanted-eyed logic guided by pleasure, pain, romance, lust, menace and fond illusion. Today, as yesterday, in the French Quarter it is thankfully okay to be flamboyant and flawed. Unquiet minds are welcome. So are stargazers and those with a stormy heart, soul, spirit and emotion; people who live head-on with fantasy and reality, illusion and truth, merging and layering themselves into a surprisingly compelling, absorbing, profound place. In the Crescent City vestiges of grandeur, culture, myth and strange serendipity abound and intertwine.

Beyond the faded walls and day-to-day struggles, New Orleanians strive to live and savor life, to mark the celebration of triumph over adversity. Taboos are few. Mirth and merriment prevail, trumping sadness. Hardships are many. Corruption and debauchery, grace and elegance meld. Rejoicing takes hold alongside mourning. Something intensely powerful persists in a crumbling city with a battered and bruised soul. The local French Quarterite can be outrageous and eccentric, a total over-the-top character yet totally clandestine, hidden in the murk and shadows beneath the cloak of anonymity. Most find this unfettered, rebellious attitude uniquely enticing and attractive, provocative and seductive, dangerous and intoxicating, inspiring and primal, impious and uncanny, cloistered and oxymoronic.

French Quarterites live with abandon in the temperamental moment yet remain firmly wedded to the specters of yesterday. It is okay to joyfully and stubbornly parade in streets, dance and sing, have a conversation or shed a tear with ancestors who sleep in the Cities of the Dead. In Louisiana the Patricians are free to sup with the sinners and saints of Bourbon Street. New Orleans, an historic locale and artistically fertile mix of stimulation with isolation is where you delve into the dark mirrors, comedies, tragedies, and intricacies of life.

Once you have lived this lifestyle and partaken of the peculiar promised land shared with scandalous and sassy people, it is impossible to relinquish the confections, concoctions, incarnations and incantations of New Orleans; few can do so, as Lafcadio Hearn said in 1876, without regret.

Welcome to the inner sanctum of our little world. Whether upright, blighted, twisted, sinking below water or turned upside down, nobody can take away who we are inside; we will survive, we will battle extinction, and we will continue to influence mankind and humanity with our unique culture. From near and far around the globe, the applause is great. All know our name and more love our city than not. Come join us for prayers in purgatory and Hail Marys in heaven, for beignets and chicory coffee and a round of cryptic cocktails and sweet madness at the edge of the earth....

40 Days, 40 Nights

{ 1 }

The path linking cathedrals to crypts is lined with the vapory secrets of sinners and saints.

*M*enace trails fond illusion.

There is no comfort in the lips of an angel, only
the suspension of time, truth and reality.

When leaders and lovers lie to us, we tend to
believe the lie even though we know it is a lie.

The truth has little charm.

We hammer at the doors of heaven and hades to let
us in, to let us go out, while the sleeping guardians
are always there, waiting to swallow us.

The ties that bind us can also blind us.

Nice people have dark and destructive urges.

The illusion of escape is what matters.

We are all lost and wandering orphans of the storm
that rages inside.

Protectors are often assailants.

What is banned and prohibited is more enjoyable
than ever.

Heroes do not reason with logic.

Cold slabs of broken stone and sanctuaries cannot
console us from the ravages of grief, for we see
what no one else can see.

What clings to our soul never washes away.

The gods give us extensions but never a full pardon.

Who you lend your heart to dictates your destiny.

Time is a liar and a thief.

Broken wings can take you far.

A man who forgets his past and allows the flame
of the things he loves to be extinguished
has no future.

We are servants of our secrets.

Sooner or later a man who cloaks himself in two
masks forgets which one is real.

We barter ourselves away in small slices.

Love is a bittersweet mystery, a misery that cures
and infects all who sup of its chalice of charm.

Not all obsession is bad.

Anger rarely goes away; it settles somewhere behind
the heart, seeping into an obscure scar.

Fate is an indiscriminate harlot.

A part of us remains in the walls and there are no
true farewells.

Survivors go where angels fear to tread.

Many things are dimming yet still ravishingly
beautiful in eternal twilight, and we are drawn
to these broken places.

Some people will eat your soul.

From the ruins comes rumination and recovery.

Promises are debts, with a price.

We know that the passage of time alters memories,
    but memories can also alter the passage of time.

Intimate enemies are the most lethal.

The mischief and memoirs of a misfit are more
    entertaining than that of a monk.

Good taste is boring.

Vices seep into our hearts as virtues in disguise.

Those who shock us interest us.

Disaster bares us, strips us of our veils, and yet
    oddly empowers us as well.

What is forbidden is most attractive.

Those broken into a million little pieces fade into
    the dust or begin again.

Passion is a perilous pursuit.

The crescent of the moon is the curve of life to
   which we hold fast.

All seek souvenirs of people, places, things, loves lost.

The stability of life is traced in the sand.

All long to embrace something larger than the
   visceral present.

The grave is our muse.

We learn to cuddle our miseries and cradle
   our albatrosses.

There is never as much time, for anything,
   as you think.

Danger and delight are inseparable.

To be alive, no matter how pretty, is to have a
   tangled and mangled life.

Foibles and follies make life interesting.

One can seldom determine when the journey
 really begins.

The moment is most real once past.

When passion dies, the stars seem dim and
 distant, the sun and moon but a mere
 shadow on the horizon.

Not every prophet possesses honor.

The condensation and soot of what no longer is,
 adheres to us.

A slice of paradise is often a slice of hell.

Rogues, renegades and rascals often live a long life.

History always takes its revenge.

Next to our most noble and loving emotions are
 our most evil emotions, and they alternate.

Men of great vision see the invisible.

Who has not had a moment of being seduced
    by madness?

The truth can make you a traitor.

Once a place touches our heart, the memory lives
    within us always.

Happy endings are not the end.

The past was so, so long ago, yet we see glimmerings
    just over the horizon.

A cowardly friend is no friend at all.

Talkers of the tongue throw the daggers of
    an assassin.

He who lives on reason alone is not wise.

The wisps of clouds are like fingers that pull us
    toward the sun like the ill-fated Icarus.

Whatever we resist will persist.

It is a dark and murky deep within the human psyche.

Most deceit is sacred and canonized.

The passage of time is sleepless, waiting to devour us;
	yet our fingerprints remain.

We love the most what we have lost.

There are many imposters, with broken smiles.

Some doors ought not to be opened.

Crash-and-burn victims litter the roads of the
	fool's paradise.

The rich have few faults.

Many of our most favorite places are dank and
	deceit-filled hideaways.

Celebrate excesses and eccentricities.

Devils in disguise are granted full entrée into
    private sanctuaries.

We are all deeply flawed.

Pity those who have yet to glimpse the edge
    of the abyss.

Hard times question integrity.

Just because something vanishes does not mean it
    never existed.

Bad people usually get what they want.

When the gods want to break a man's heart, they
    give him a lot of intelligence and good sense.

Even devils have regrets.

What rides in on a thin pink cloud usually
    evaporates as quickly as it came.

Throw tantrums, often.

It is the dry embers and ashes of old fires that
smolder and burn deeply in the soul, branding
and scarring us forever.

The ominous attracts us.

All memories recede to a flicker behind closed eyes.

Sweet lullabies corrupt, fairytales lie and mislead.

Even palace and fortress walls crumble.

We all serve a prison sentence deep within the
dungeon of our inner self.

To find reality, search for unicorns.

Resist a handmaiden's help.

We all curl up into ourselves, vanishing into a
dreamy hothouse of languid memories beyond
the mangled mist, mingled with the fragrance
of soft decay.

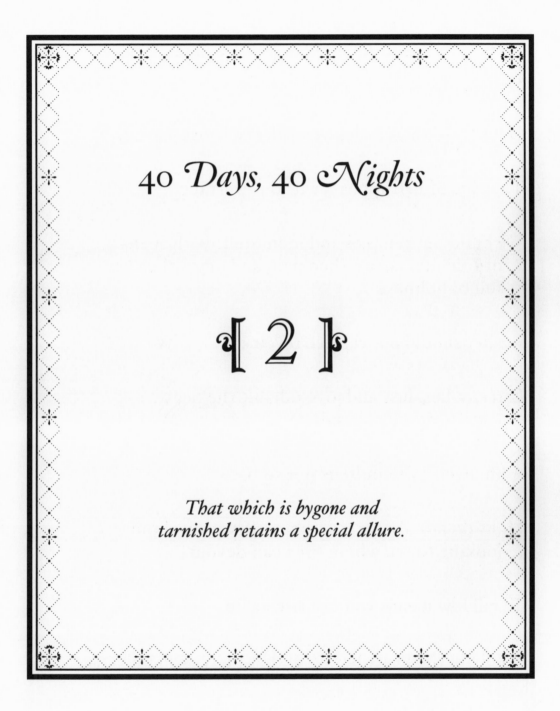

40 Days, 40 Nights

❬ 2 ❭

*That which is bygone and
tarnished retains a special allure.*

Nobody pulls through the storm unscathed.

Out of the black hole, we stalk the beast within.

The face of hell appears without warning.

We build our temples and memorials with spells
    of splendor, astonished pain and empty bricks
    full of holiness.

Reality should not replace revelry.

Larceny, lies, lust and love inhabit the heart,
    coexisting side-by-side.

A life lived by impulse is not so bad.

Lions do not always roar when they walk about
    looking to see whom they can devour.

To fall low means you can rise again.

A hole in the heart has no end; it pierces all universes.

Legends frighten fools.

There is much we would like to forget, but, short
of amnesia, we never forget these things.

Sometimes we live as a consequence.

All humans are stained with the taint of
malevolence, vanity and falsehood.

Satan is never satisfied.

It is better to be despised for what you are than to
be adored for what you are not.

Fend off protocol, bend and break the rules.

To be drawn to tackiness, like a moth to a flame,
is freeing.

Impending doom is often irrevocable.

What is adored can suddenly become abhorrent.

The mouth of self-indulgence is never sated.

We seek and find a strange comfort in what is
familiar, even pain.

Calamity is not always unexpected.

Deprivation and desperation build desire, as do
delusion and dementia.

Everyone touches the void.

All masterpieces are fractured, in some way, eventually.

The timid never know victory or defeat.

Daunting, haunting, taunting memories can never
be flung into the fire, not really.

The ravages of time take their toll.

Some bonds cannot be explained or broken.

To follow the haphazard road and journey is the
most exciting.

It is impossible to move on without looking back.

Cruelty is born of weakness.

Never let a psychotic master charmer of the soul
    stake a claim on your psyche.

Time punishes all things.

No matter where we live or take shelter, in the end
    it is all pried from us.

Defy convention.

It is a fault to be too perfect.

We bear the inequities, curses and sorrows of those
    whom we love.

Some secrets cannot be sanitized.

It is comforting and calming to believe we endure,
    to be attached to the idea of fate and destiny.

Fools feast and fester on folly.

Conquistadors and adventurers are envied by many.

Woe brings innovation.

A person's true essence is the impact he or she
     leaves on others.

What we exalt, we tear down.

The road to ruin is an enticingly fragrant path,
     with a great view.

It is hidden wrath that charms.

What is garish, crumpled and withered can also
     be beautiful.

Malice has a deep memory.

There are tragic, lost survivors everywhere —
     not easily recognizable.

A deceiver deceives himself.

People who inhabit a world of protective edifices
     hide many secrets that outsiders are not
     permitted to observe.

Life is a legend of lies.

Crushed hearts smash into debris like scattered
particles of dust.

A liar's lair knows no boundaries.

It is difficult to avoid the bittersweet pleasure of
being an injustice collector.

Angst is at times an asset.

The stealthy monster within consumes those
who dabble too deep in ambition and a quest
for power.

Who rests in peace?

The worst demon is one who damns, crucifies and
kills our dreams.

Nobody escapes the sting of betrayal.

Our fates collide and dovetail, whether we like it
or not.

It is better to fight than to forget.

That which is provocative is also offensive, with
    curative powers.

Envy emanates through the eyes.

Faceless stalkers always stand in wait, in the near
    distance just out of reach, somewhere at the
    edge of the horizon.

Silence suffocates.

Kings, queens and conquerors have all known the
    sting of evil, jealousy and wisdom.

A dark descent knows no limits.

Sleep is the remedy for fear.

The refugee of life always holds dear in his or her
    damaged head images of the broken home of
    their heart, the ruined soil that they still love;
    a land where their spirit soars and lives.

Empires are made of dirt.

Devil dust is usually tasty.

The long arm of fate is considered significantly
    stronger, more lethal, and far-reaching than the
    long arm of the law could ever be.

Cynicism breeds decadence.

There is solace at the edge.

We curl up tight to fend off the cold island of day.

Many promises crumble easily.

The only way to preserve the kaleidoscope that is
    life is to forever keep it in motion.

Rubble and broken glass sharpen the senses.

We sometimes catch glimpses and vestiges of
    things gone by, all that has preceded us.

Nothing is ours to keep forever.

The laws of gravity do not apply to love or real life.

Yesterday never dies.

Bad luck can take you on a course you never
dreamed of.

Mixed motives lurk behind every mask.

Only monkeys and fools see, hear, speak and
do no evil.

We all stir the ashes of discontent.

Death, power, pain and struggle reemerge like
clockwork, the big questions of life demanding
to be embraced.

Rebels and mutineers make history.

Hope is a hazardous pastime.

It is not uncommon to sleep with angels and run
with devils.

A prayer for salvation and the guilt of a survivor
never fade from memory; no, those memories
never leave you, no matter how many times
people tell you that you had no choice.

Fear is a cruel master.

The fidelity of friends is questionable.

Everyone has sunk in a sea of emotion, and love,
strange and warped.

Tombs swelter with secrets.

Magic and mystery stir a man's blood.

It is sometimes difficult to determine whether one
is standing inside or outside the circle of hell;
the line is permeable, blurry and moveable.

Evil smiles are found in high places.

The voice of rumor travels far.

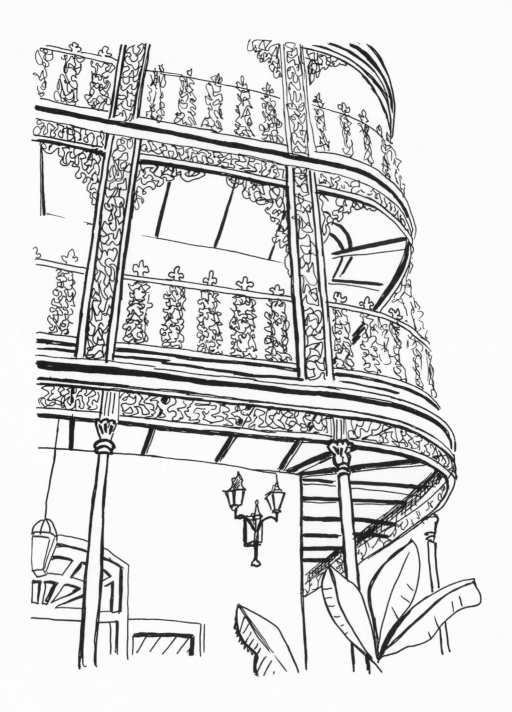

40 Days, 40 Nights

{ 3 }

*One day can erase hundreds
of years of history.*

We all wonder, how do I slay the dragon in me?

Time does not heal, it just quiets us.

Words upon the windowpane call out to us, but
    sometimes we ignore their summons; we do
    not want to hear what is spoken and unspoken.

Cinderella stories usually go terribly wrong.

Tainted voices speak much; sometimes even
    the truth.

Many merchants of misery go unrecognized.

A heart with no nostalgia or regret, erased of
    reminiscences, belongs to a liar or has never
    known love or loss.

Live it up, life is over in a finger snap.

Faith sometimes blinds our eyes and blackens
    our hearts.

We all search for Eden, and the vanishing light.

Most inquisitors and hypocrites live with molten
    skeletons rotting in their fragile houses.

It is better to be right than reasonable.

Happiness and sadness are held in the same hand.

Mockery carries some truth.

Who has not longed to go back in time, if only
    for a moment — to right a wrong; to see, hear,
    feel and touch someone again; to say, I am sorry,
    I love you, forgive me?

Only blind men live in a blissful world.

The past is a foreign country, a trunk full
    of memories.

Even Camelot has a dark side.

Self-inflicted wounds are the most painful and take
    the longest to heal.

We all inhabit the kingdom of deception.

In an impermanent world of change, man gathers his
strength from history, fables, fairytales and romance.

Dark rage often hides behind a smile.

Secrets revealed and spilled can never be wiped up
and put into their place.

Desire and fear govern the world.

Raucous, violent, happy, crazy places are the
most exciting.

All comfort is false.

Remnants of memories are but puzzle pieces,
imagery that continually breaks apart only to
reform again in new ways.

We are more resilient than we imagine.

Sleepless nights are many for those who search for
hope and meaning in the abandonment of life.

A sordid past can be sexy.

When the rollercoaster stops you disembark at the
bottom, not the top.

The souls meet on the lips.

If one is lucky, a sea of irresistible sweet misery lies
between cradle and coffin.

We are all weak and mortal.

The eyes, head and heart are all capable of such
great deceit.

Excess is best.

Riches crumble, decay, evaporate and vanish, far
too quickly and easily.

Destruction comes swiftly.

Fortune owes us nothing just because she took
back what she loaned us.

Unquiet minds are provocative.

Buttoned-up pious perfection can explode
    into wantonness.

Feckless fate is a friend, a foe, a fiend.

A dark mirror reflects upon those who live in
    gilded cages.

There is peril and splendor in bad behavior.

Heroes and villains both dance to the devil's violin,
    waltzing as one.

Lies are sometimes the truth in masquerade.

Some believe it just to live by a Homeric code of
    honor, loyalty and revenge.

We are all dancing in the dark.

Staring deep into the abyss is an intriguing pastime.

No road is without regret.

It is wise to listen to the voice of the voiceless.

Murmurs and failures lead us into and out
of the flames.

Reconciliation is hard to pick over revenge.

Fortune favors the bold.

Even fabled people are swept up in the flow of
time, eroded.

Humanity is manacled to itself whether we like it
or not.

The good times always move; the party ends.

We fear being dropped into the darkness where we
plunge and plummet alone, hopefully to resurface.

Most liars lie with logic.

A veil of moonlight glosses, softens and blurs the
seams and edges of all things good and bad.

Life is a charade.

We look for something to do, for someone with
    whom to share our miseries.

You rarely get what you sacrifice for.

The worth of a man's life is the love and good deeds
    he leaves behind in the wake of his memory.

Fear gives wings to courage.

The mercurial emperors and circles of life erupting
    are timeless.

A life devoid of passion is a life poorly lived.

Money matters, particularly to the fine art of
    survival, greed and madness.

Heaven and hell both lie.

Life spews its tragedies and moments of glory at us.

Intriguing people have a past and a presence.

The undertows of our inward sea lap quietly at us,
    dragging us straight into deep raging waters,
    way over our heads.

Some voids cannot be filled.

The dearly departed are never wholly forgotten;
    nor do the ghosts of yesterday slumber soundly.

Nobody can explain us to ourselves.

Question everything.

The pieces of ourselves that we give away and
    surrender to the world are more important than
    the possessions we cling to, the idols we worship,
    or the things that possess us.

Catastrophe and success often run side-by-side.

The winding ways of the heart often usher us to
    profane places, illicit liaisons.

Everyone enjoys gossip.

The clamorous need to be loved bedevils us.

Who is not possessed and tortured by the fire
    within, whether a spark or a raging inferno?

Trust is more important than belief.

In the dimness of nighttime unleashed, pent-up
    fear, rage and smoldering secrets run rampant.

Being sensible makes no sense at all.

The voice of reason and the voice of intuition
    seldom agree. Follow your instinct.

Sunken treasures sometimes reemerge.

Mayhem rains down upon us, but it can be misery
    or mirth.

Truth and trauma are illusive.

Once cut, do not continue to crawl across
    broken glass.

Embrace disaster, as we must.

Wars are never won, not really.

The age-old ironies of agonies and ecstasies, of
    grief and gala, go hand-in-hand.

Perfection is bland and characterless.

Time is fluid.

Even in the bleakest days, disillusionment
    sometimes precedes a reawakening, readying us
    to respond to life's challenges.

Placid heroes are camouflaging something.

Some people relish ravenous takedowns and
    blood sports.

Payback time is coiled and convoluted.

Monsters live in the mirror.

40 Days, 40 Nights

[4]

Trouble lands at everyone's door.

*L*essons to be learned are rarely remembered.

Something is always about to be taken from us,
   leaving in its place what is indefinite, unfamiliar
   and unknown.

Only brave eyes are willing to probe our
   tormented world.

A lonely hurt is more painful than a shared one.

Every devil has not a cloven hoof.

Tricksters and martyrs are often one in the same
   and difficult to distinguish.

Song, dance and celebration are all a part of the
   healing process.

Nobody can take away what lies deep within.

We imprison ourselves in our own locked
   velvet rooms.

Guilty pleasures gratify.

People with few vices have few virtues.

When it comes to a twilight tango dance with
    mortality, the human spirit can handle
    almost anything.

The destination is never what you think.

Reckonings and remedies can be fatal.

We see the clearest when we lie awake in the
    starless night envisioning all we wish to forget.

In life, there is no bottom.

Phantoms of sundown chase us, and yet run from us.

Survivors make friends with shadows.

It is not always easy to recognize the hell hounds
    that guard the gates to the underworld.

What is revealed is not always visible.

It is best to never see the guillotine blade poised
above your neck.

The restlessness inside is hardest to tame.

When life breaks you and sensibilities crumble,
one can still dance, love and fight.

Despair is a vulture that consumes us.

We all pursue the past. It stalks us.

The laughing faces of yesterday come and go
before us.

We all want forever.

Deep, devious, mysterious secrets and lies,
shimmering in the sun, lurking in the shadows,
camouflage the decay that hides behind the
gloss, revealing that nothing is as it seems.

The mind is full of false memories.

Live incidentally.

People awash in crises are always the most
  unforgettable, vivid and gripping.

Great piety fosters hypocrisy.

Many families have a cold, dark side.

Some of the best men lie upon the straw of failure.

The more condensed the loss and pain, the deeper
  it burns.

Splendor is a short-lived reign.

Most lairs and liars look beautiful until you
  are trapped.

The heart is the impetuous ruler of the soul.

Is the pleasure of having something worth the pain
  of losing it?

We leave the past in the dust, so we think, but old
  sandstorms still overtake us.

All of life is but a makeshift raft, tossed high and
   low, amid crashing waves and tormented seas;
   sometimes we ride the crest and feel the sun
   upon our face, sometimes we dip below,
   underwater, only to disappear quietly into
   the choppy darkness.

None are immune to an uncertain future.

All humans have demons.

The truths that come easily in the dark of night are
   sometimes hard to coax out into the light of day.

Fear destroys all, weak and strong alike.

To embrace power one must be prepared to brush
   off the hazards.

Private sorrows sear, yet strengthen the soul.

Behind each secret lurks a truth, and often a sacrifice.

There is malice in wonderland.

Honeyed voices frequently hide a poisonous darkness.

Man's confessionals vanish into thin air.

The fine fog in our consciousness reveals many
truths, covering us like a mist, whether we like
it or not.

We are patriots and traitors.

Love and liquor make you old and gray, but it may
be worth it.

Who has not been kissed by a poisoned rose?

The odyssey of a century can occur in a day.

When you say too much, nobody hears, listens or
remembers.

People do have a right to their beliefs and opinions,
even if ridiculous.

Authority is not always right.

If we are lucky, a little wisp of our memory gets passed from one to another like a dimming flambeau flame, and we leave a light, perhaps a kindled fire.

The lust for power is rooted in weakness.

What is wrong and righteous is irreparably intertwined.

The urge to fly away is always strong.

Sometimes we live to mourn.

Funerals are for those left behind, not the dearly departed.

We dredge through the deluge of life.

Seductive eyes glisten with secrets.

The sway of vermillion lips and the sensation of angel breath swirl and suck many into the heart of depravity.

Old wounds are easily opened.

Few are not frightened by change, humility and shame.

Capricious nature is both cruel and kind.

What lives in the mind and heart remains
    alive, always.

Time belies, twists and yet tells the truth.

Who you love is more important than whom you
    hate; so long as they do not meld into one and
    the same.

Power arouses amoral moments.

The wise see stars through the mud, angels in
    the mire.

Provocative is scary, and scary is provocative.

It is what you do not want to know that will come
    back to haunt you.

Foolhardy romantics can become deranged.

The happiest ask no questions, seek no answers.

Nothing escapes the dust of time.

The gods help and hinder us.

Many misfits step from the shadows to manipulate
and surmount the world.

Danger and fairytales are both bittersweet.

To live a storybook life requires one to be a
storyteller.

Life's impermanence is a bitter pill.

A great fortune paves the way to great slavery.

The crackle of nighttime beckons us.

One moment can determine your entire life, then
the moment is gone.

High drama and near tragedy are fickle friends.

When you think you have a tiger by the tail,
    and you are the one in control, the truth is,
    what you might actually have hold of is nothing
    but a sneaky, slippery, coiled serpent, a snake
    capable of slithering out of your grasp, then
    springing around and nailing you with a pair
    of sharp, lethal fangs.

The road to victory is the road to defeat.

Battles come when least expected.

When the air is heavy, oppressive and humid,
    be careful.

The greatest instinct is survival.

Be careful to whom you confess.

Every gift comes with a whip.

40 Days, 40 Nights

[5]

*Live on the edge,
and do not look down.*

Reality is always tarnished.

The storm surges pull us under.

Life is a gathering of souls huddled as though in a
    drawing room of contrasts and the unexpected,
    and always at the edge of the abyss.

In a laughter-and-tear-soaked life of stains and
    scars, amid the customs, rituals, fires, ashes and
    waters of time, who is to say what is what,
    which is which?

Fallen angels fly the highest.

It is unwise and ill-advised to be overly civil.

Everyone wrestles with, against and over the
    scruples of principles and powers.

Sinister terrain beckons us all.

You can run away as fast as you can, but there is no
    escape from the ties and chains that bind us.

Provocateurs rule.

The scale of a man's possessions do not make
    the man.

People with the most rules have the least mercy.

There is misfortune in too much virtue.

Echoes of the people we have loved and lost,
    destroyed and abandoned along the way, whisper
    in our ears; forever reminding us of what was
    and yet will never be.

Borrow from an angel, repay a devil.

Peace of mind comes slowly, usually in old age,
    if ever at all.

He who thinks he knows, does not know.

No matter how sordid the nightmare, there are
    those who choose to believe in fairytales, love
    and the power of redemption.

Silenced thoughts turn rebellious.

The nectar of the gods can be perilous to
  mere mortals.

Many are blinded by their own brilliance.

Showmen and shamans often share the same soul.

Paradise is always in peril.

Only madmen recognize society's faults.

Sooner or later all things precious fragment and
  fall apart.

Ashes can reemerge as aspirations.

Only the brave are willing to divulge glimpses of
  hurt, raw and painful.

Deprivation inspires desire.

Beauty is very deceitful.

Most wonderments of the world, including love,
    cannot be explained or proven, just accepted or not.

Thin, moveable gossamer lines divide fact and
    fabrication, myth and reality.

Some hide behind the shell of an empty soul.

What is tragic is also mysterious and interesting.

All life is distorted.

Our stories become more real than living man.

It is never easy to walk hand-in-hand with the
    distorted reflections of yesterday while
    confronting the hounds of hell that nip at
    our heels today.

You can never level the wind.

Even the desperate, desolate and lonely have a voice.

The celebration of life is lived to the max by
    straddling the precipice.

The mind creates with pain.

Not all fear the dark side of humanity.

Everyone dies, but not everyone lives.

It is impossible to silence the "little voice" that
    lurks inside us.

We are drawn to Greek tragedies.

The most intriguing people and places come wrapped
    in splendor and decay, riches and corrosion.

Crisis brings danger and opportunity.

Never confess.

Sirens whisper their bittersweet songs of lullaby to
    those who will listen.

We all sacrifice little pieces of ourselves.

To follow one's innermost impulses is the best way
    to survive the passage of time and disaster.

Life is tethered in hope and endurance, in history
and culture, in romance and despair, in sorrow
and celebrations.

A shy demeanor can conceal a spine of steel.

Once the veil is lifted, it is more difficult to
believe in triumph over sorrow, in the promise
beyond failure.

Who anoints wise men wise?

Some regrets and guilts are immeasurable
and untraceable.

Loveliness and honesty rarely agree.

The gateway between paradise and perdition, truth
and lies, happiness and misery is divided by but
a hair's breath.

Six feet under makes all equal.

Everyone has a cryptic side, the moon within,
which is not shown to others.

A bully is a coward behind a mask.

Only dead people have no pain, bear no burdens.

Principles are the first thing sacrificed.

When we look back at our life, our wildest
escapades are the most memorable; they make
us smile when life's miseries, sepulchers and
bitter wailings conspire to humble us.

All that is known is not told.

Caution is best viewed backwards, through the
shrouded twilight of resurrection.

Nobody cheats fate.

Flaunt your true colors.

Not all hunters announce their presence with the
blow of a horn.

We often believe against all evidence.

If you do not stand for something, you stand
for nothing.

Closure is always illusive and rarely final.

All yearn to tumble down the rabbit hole into
wonderland.

It can never be made right.

Fables, folklore and fairytales have a stronger
influence on us, imprinted on the fabric of
daily life.

Those tested by life learn to be shameless.

We hear half-forgotten melodies, touch
half-burned embers, sing words we cannot
remember, with the promise of yesterday
receding in the vanished distance of invisible
vapor wet with tears.

Shady daredevils on the edge skirt death best.

Greed changes everything, putting all at grave risk.

Restless hearts and scorched souls gravitate to
sweet poison.

There are perils in aiming for sainthood.

Sometimes we sink when we think we are climbing.

The past chips the edge of truth.

If we pass the line, the time and place, of no
return, we become a stranger in our life, our
own skin, and a shadow of who we once were.

Life rarely proceeds as planned.

Bars are the best places to overhear stories and
legends of lost dreams.

Chaos and its offspring rule the world.

We are drawn to the cryptic corners of human
nature and impenetrable people.

A view from the top is not always pretty.

And then it all turns to dust, designating upon our raw fingertips as we try to hold tight.

It is hard to let go of lost worlds.

Those on patrol mark their fate more prominently than those who cower.

Great choices are made by accident.

The human heart digs into the past as an anchor.

Dreams should never be relinquished to the authorities of life.

Majorities are often mistaken.

Be an instigator.

The muse of what is long gone and no more, that which will never be touched again, remains forever locked in the head.

40 Days, 40 Nights

{ 6 }

*It is okay to have a conversation
or shed a tear with ancestors who
sleep in the Cities of the Dead.*

*W*isdom does not produce courage.

In time most everything turns to ash, floating
away, slipping from our fingers.

A beacon of doubt is better than a watchtower
of certainty.

To spar with Satan sharpens the reflexes.

A consuming heat burns at the outer limits of the
dark side of the mind.

Logic does not always make sense.

Many step blindsighted and slip-slide deeper into
the sleaze.

Ecstasy and agony come together as pairs.

Faceless people send others to do their bidding, to pull
the soiled strings that they hold and control.

Men create many gods in their own image.

People believe most what they least understand.

The fire of a heretic is contagious.

Control is a tricky illusion; we are never in charge
the way we think.

Destiny is a merciless mistress.

Few can tell the difference between the beauty
of good and the ugliness of evil.

Grief never washes away.

The heart-stain is always there.

Lust, love, lies, hate and greed help the world spin
on its axis.

We weep for our greatest delight.

Some depths of murky madness are places from
which there is no return.

The truth is too heavy for most to bear.

When trapped in a place called holy hell, inner
demons dance with guardian angels.

Swashbucklers sup with saints and sinners.

To bathe in magic and mystery one must loosen the
senses, sharpen the mind, taste the shredded
confetti of ethos, mythos and pathos.

Everything passes away, including time.

In the veil of shadows, prying evil eyes cannot
stare a tender soul into oblivion.

Fear the calm, enjoy the storm.

Many things are more dreadful than they seem.

The devil's boots tread as softly as moccasins.

As the sand escapes from our hourglass of life,
sometimes we see clearer.

Death is unequivocal.

The most toxic of all falsehoods is the slightly
distorted half-truth.

Wrinkles are written upon the brow, not the heart.

A trail of tears helps to drown the pain.

Some mysteries should be lived and enjoyed,
not solved.

False courage can take you far.

We often pry open the door into a grotto of lies.

Silver-tongued serpents move in a circle.

Just below the surface, deep shades of unleashed
disarray may be detected.

Shining swords impale and stake the soul.

The implications are rarely as clear as they
might seem.

Desperation awakens contempt.

Take illusion and pleasure into your own hands.

Hope keeps the heart from breaking.

It is impossible to ever know if you are on the
right road.

Even mockers are undone in time.

To delve into the turmoil of what lies beneath is to
run in looped circles.

Debts are lessons.

Best friends are often prone to be meddling,
ungrateful, arrogant, dishonest, jealous, resentful
and surly.

We drink in bitterness every day.

The betrayal of a friend is harder to forgive than
enemy warfare.

Rumor is the mother of revolution.

Grudges lodge deep and are difficult to dislocate.

Melancholy in the heart is the seat of perdition.

Forbidden and secret enticements have the
    strongest charm.

Who has not marinated in failure?

To live a long life requires an extended passage
    through the valley of evil, suffering, loss
    and anguish.

Myths are facts in disguise.

The cruelest lies are most often spread and
    planted in silence.

A good name often loses its luster after dark.

Revenge is a consequence, concession and
    confession of pain.

Truth is a child born of time.

Fortune knocks loudly to announce its arrival;
    misfortune quietly sneaks in the back door.

Great men are not necessarily wise.

Those with a weakness for praise often succumb
    to temptation.

Without nightmares, there could be no dreams.

Incorrigible and inescapable remembrances that
    we hold inside ourselves, invisible to others,
    hurt and heal our heads and hearts.

Never let your possessions fall heavy upon
    your shoulders.

We are all humbled by the darkness.

It takes a traitor to fool a Judas.

We can be in limbo and tatters, unraveling at an
    alarming rate, yet we pretend to be in control.

Long-held secrets eventually wither away.

Neither the past nor future can be lost, only the
present, as we cannot lose what we do not have.

False friendship is a sword in the back.

Even the good are afflicted with malice, cunning
and hypocrisy.

The other side of sorrow is steep.

When the soft decay of the hanging gardens creeps
in, some come to hail the splendor and statues
of Babylon.

Everyone needs a Socrates.

True love will fight and conquer heaven and hell,
angels and devils.

It is easy to be shoved, pushed or pulled into
the abyss.

All things are impermanent, except change.

Hope does not always bring glory.

We all mask ourselves, and live amid a world of mistaken identities.

Over and over again we willfully and purposefully torture ourselves by reconstructing the shadowy etchings of painful memories.

The murk of mystery is irresistible.

Like seeks like, yet the allure of opposites attracts and ignites.

The irrational can always be rationalized.

Ultimately, many wands are waved and webs spun.

Leave room for chance.

Those who follow the rules, who go by the book and think only in black and white, do not move or lead the world.

Silent fools can pass for wise.

Wrinkles are the scrapbook of life.

In time, we are moving away, splitting, into the
backward flow.

Pain and suffering, grief, healing and redemption,
consume one in the blaze — yet leave behind
some small measure of wisdom, and insight.

Tomorrow is today, and yesterday.

Live hard, play hard, as to be at peace and unity
with the world and its afterlife is not really
possible, for mere mortals.

Scattered tears sometimes build a stream to the
long-lost invisible river of happiness.

What you see is not always what you think.

Storybook settings are deceiving.

The devil can cite scripture and build spires better
than angels.

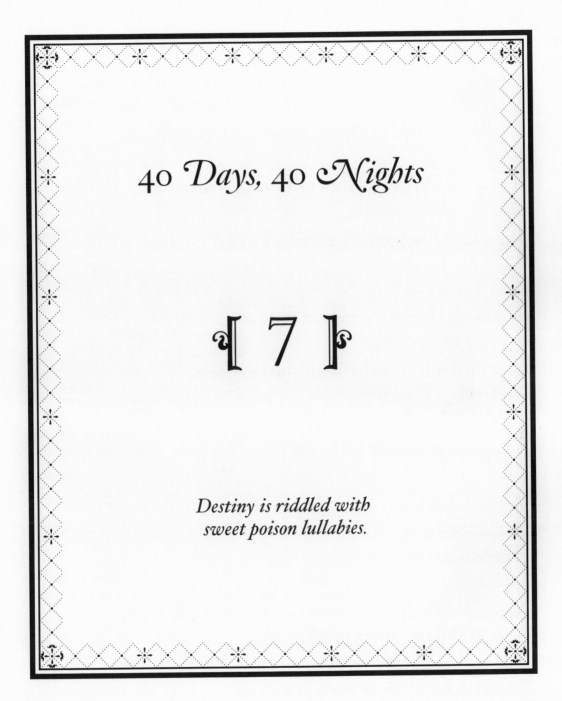

40 Days, 40 Nights

[7]

Destiny is riddled with
sweet poison lullabies.

*D*efeat is never final.

Madhouses and madmen are indeed engrossing.

The prism of enchantment is always distorted.

Symbols of defiance are badges of honor, marks
of distinction.

Loves and loyalties are not always compatible.

It is difficult to swim with the tin gods
without drowning.

The voyage within is the cure.

A mind at large is a wonderfully scary thing to unleash.

There is an inferno inside.

We go down into the ravines of wretchedness to
find the treasures of life.

Sometimes we close our eyes to see.

Only fools and madmen willingly voyage into
    the underworld.

Every crypt is a silent story.

Forked tongues slice deeper than any knife.

We are a slave to kicking against fate and
    mistrusting the future.

Beautiful demons and disasters are compelling.

Nobody is untouched by tragedy.

Some muses are memorable enough to haunt and
    bewitch our waking and sleeping hours.

Raconteurs rule.

Utopia is never found where you think, and is
    never as you envision it.

Dissolute darkness is very attractive.

Time is saturated with broken lives.

Life is rarely set in concrete; the course can be changed, if you know how.

The truth is always murky.

Humanity sometimes hides behind our façade.

The fragments of our lives rarely blend seamlessly; they remain jagged and ragged, painful to touch and remember.

Scandalous people are stirring.

Those from the past see us as we were, a face from long ago that no longer exists.

Unauthorized anarchy is good.

The truth enslaves.

Answer to no one.

Tenderness and sadness usually intersect with the sinister and wise.

Success and failure, pain and pleasure, wealth and
    poverty, all of these, and more, happen to good
    and evil alike; so they are neither noble nor
    shameful, neither good nor bad.

Invariably there are stories behind the stories.

We hold onto the people and things we have loved
    as eternal pictures in our mind.

Injustice is power.

Great fortune is tied to great misfortune.

There are always secrets long buried in the past,
    waiting to be discovered.

It is sometimes good to forget what you know.

When an old world disappears, a new one begins.

Life is a dream and a nightmare.

The unwritten often reveals more than what
    is written.

Not every question requires an answer.

What inspires you can destroy you.

Life moves in the rotating circlet of ageless
    crowns of thorns and handcuffs of diamonds,
    everything reoccurring.

Everyone is both master and servant.

The wanton greed, hunger and thirst of the angel
    of death know no end, no boundaries; the
    catabolic angel is never satisfied, never filled.

Portraits of loss are not always obvious.

Sometimes the gods step in with slicing humor
    and harm.

That which soars also plummets.

We are all vulnerable to pain, arrogance and meanness.

People can be heroes and villains simultaneously.

There is always poison in paradise.

Reckless lives are sometimes well spent, as they do not always crash and burn.

What is treasured is always on the tightropes.

Blasphemy commonly occurs during scavenger hunts for rich treasures, and on long journeys in search of the oracle of truth.

Uncovering old strife leads to new hatred.

It is best to always see for yourself, to step back far enough to take in the whole picture.

Shared memories help us transcend suffering.

People are canonized for what they believe and crucified for what they know.

To embrace and to conquer is not the same thing.

Most twists of fate are memorable in hindsight.

Impressionism combats despair.

The darkest hours of tragedy and devastation bring
    forth what is inside us, whether it be intensity
    or nothingness.

A life well lived embraces the edge of chaos.

The biggest battle between good and evil takes
    place inside.

A hungry heart is never satisfied.

Once faced with the dark side of life, there is more
    revel in joy.

Disappointment is the handmaiden of wisdom.

Myth and strange serendipity abound and intertwine,
    for those able to peer beyond the void.

Those that know all, pardon all.

Words set loose that cannot be reclaimed sweep us
    into a vortex of liquid fire.

Life is as random as the roulette wheel.

Most things horrid and harrowing hold a special
  morbid appeal.

Those who have known pain know how to inflict
  it, cleverly so.

You can tell a lion by its claws.

The surest road to hell is the unseen one; slow and
  steady, with a soft and gentle slope, with seemingly
  sure footing and no hairpin curves; devoid of
  warnings and guideposts.

We are never severed from the past.

The logic of the heart is usually quite illogical.

Doubt nourishes the suckling of jealousy.

The art of surface sacrifice, surrender and the
  stiffness of old scars interlace as one.

Deadly sins often pass as social virtues.

Scrape the surface to see, deception and unnamed
    psychological mind games and rot reign supreme.

Adversity exposes many truths.

Dismiss preconceived notions and be unpredictable.

Where there is envy, there is madness.

Time tames all things.

We latch onto and are lured by that which makes
    us feel something.

Indulgence is better than practicality.

When given the opportunity, live large and colorful
    with flamboyance and flair.

Every truth has two faces or more.

The wrath of sorrow fills the skies.

Life grants you a limited number of perfect days.

What the heart knows, the head may never understand.

The silence of sealed lips breeds tyranny.

Fits of bravery often spring from the frightened,
    not the fearless.

The unknown can bring extreme terror or delight.

Our shifting lives are a pendulum of holy and
    unholy ruin and recovery.

Hell is full of triangles and mocking eyes in
    the mirror.

We love most what we have lost or nearly lost,
    what vanishes now and what is long vanished.

The glare of glitter is powerful.

A basin of tears makes for a lowland of laughter, as
    the more we laugh the less we cry.

40 Days, 40 Nights

{8}

Life is written on water.

$\mathcal{M}$oney removes most stains.

Beyond the dark-jewel guises and disguises, we
    dance and make merry with intimate shadows.

The past comes to us like the tides; it ebbs and
    flows but never goes away.

We long for another time we have never known,
    for a place where enduring paradise is still ours.

Some angers and hurts can never be purged.

Troublemakers change the world.

It is normal to seek the truth beyond the
    masquerade and façade.

Character is revealed in the dark.

Misty elegances and decadences mix well together.

No life avoids detours and dreams deferred.

The bonfire of the heart and a rage behind the
 eyes are not always seen.

Southwest of purgatory lies the barren landscape
 of the heart.

In the end, the journey is all you have.

The temporal moment remains firmly wedded to
 the specters of yesterday.

So many cries are unheard, struggles untold
 and unknown.

Treachery looms in unexpected places.

It is not uncommon to have the common sense of
 table salt.

Do not like to be told what to think, ever.

The greatest gulf is in the head.

All life has a secret sordid underbelly.

The most fascinating people are distinguished
    by eccentric attitudes, odd mindsets and
    outlandish stances.

Love is more than a lyric.

Always seek to explore and fan the flames, the bliss
    and torture of the human existence.

Life grows amid the garden of the departed.

The mystics are often right.

People of influence and graft are most engaging,
    as are grifters.

To tell the truth is sometimes a perilous folly.

Is it any wonder the wise weep without shame?

Unholy passions make for unholy alliances.

The moneyed find the characters that live on the
    frayed fringes of fine society to be fetching and
    frightening, repellant and messianic.

We run with the circle of shadows that stalk us.

All life penetrates the veil of a double perspective.

The memory lies.

Who does not have a fear — of abandonment, of
    love, of living, of new beginnings, of old endings,
    of the unknown, of death?

The mythology of our past colors all.

When the gods answer our prayers, they smite us.

Both happiness and evil are as illusive as a whiff
    of smoke.

The romantic, dreamy, stormy, sad or troubled
    setting provides the transcendental key to
    reflections of another sensuous time and place.

Life is best seen through the eyes of the heart.

When troubles are few, dreams are few.

Soulless is the Sphinx, fixed for ages with silent
shadows, faceless phantoms and the cobwebs
of the mind.

We all kiss and tamper with the tangled threads
of perdition.

There is no resurrection of a disintegrated heart.

Forked shadows, twisted secrets, castles aglow at
the rim of hell-fire are all attractive.

The passage of time scrambles all with a lingering
inscription of symbolism, mystery and melancholy.

Yesterday is on the horizon, unwritten.

Neon lights, dark moons dawning, and shadows in the
sun bring us to the other side of the lower world.

The depths of a rift can rarely be reversed, except
on the surface.

No one is without loss.

The twisted terms of fate bring us to our knees.

What you worship can predict your woe.

The remnants of regret and remorse linger;
    sweepings of the past burrow and hide deep yet
    remain impossible to ignore.

Hatreds are the cinders of losses and loves.

To be alive is to embrace the pain of day, the desire
    of night.

A ray of darkness touches and permeates
    everything, searching for the light.

The venom and fire of an open wound, in time,
    form a thin, fragile scar that festers and oozes
    from the vindictiveness beneath.

We all walk blindly into the sunset, the dawn
    behind us.

The war within is rarely won.

Only the strong, romantic, rebellious and foolish
    swim against the torrents, sometimes drowning
    in bottomless open waters, yet often changing
    the world and history.

The dead open the eyes of the living.

Sometimes only a frail covering of thin skin keeps
    a soul from ripping apart.

The sheer threads that silently and thinly tether
    can also strangle.

Change is inevitable.

Who will save the saviors?

The road to paradise and purgatory follows a circle,
    with no escape.

When it comes to the peccadilloes of politics,
    love and war, rules do not apply; in this arena,
    you would think there is no right or wrong,
    no good or bad.

Heartbreak will always take you by surprise.

The confusion never ends; the truth is an
ever-changing riddle with no answer, no
beginning, and no end.

Magic is potent.

The ghosts that inhabit our mind do not sleep
soundly; they are always out there somewhere,
just a hair's breath away, soft silhouettes,
shadows in the sun.

And the crimson rain comes falling down.

We most often encounter our destiny along the
footpath we take to escape it.

The inconspicuous details are not infrequently the
most important.

It is impossible to reason with the stars and deal
with the gods.

There is no solitude or solace in silence.

What you salvage from the ruins means something
to your life.

Sweet nectar seduces us to other places.

The ache, desire, burning embers and thrill of a
    memory stay with us for a lifetime — freshly
    rewritten and colored with each passage of time.

We are all seekers, sages and spiritual pilgrims.

Most victories are hollow.

It takes a daring commitment and great passion to
    bring the promise and shadow of untold visions
    and stories to light.

Reinvention is the best revenge.

An avenging fire, turbulence in the soul maddened
    by wrongs, is sometimes good.

Life can be ruthless, unbearably so.

Familiarity, no matter how ugly or profane, always
    is, in a way, strangely comforting.

Whispers and shadows leave time in the dark.

Moral decay is often wedded to wide-eyed innocence.

Few things are worse than hypocrisy.

It is sometimes good to bury your head in the
shifting silt of a make-believe world.

Success brings no guarantee of glory.

What is fragile can also be ferocious; what is
ferocious can also be tender.

The only way to understand life is through contrast.

Barren and damaged landscapes — filled with
haunting and melancholic images of ruined
idylls, deserted and broken — hold down the
burdens of the world.

The past erupts into the present.

We can wake up stranded in a strange world.

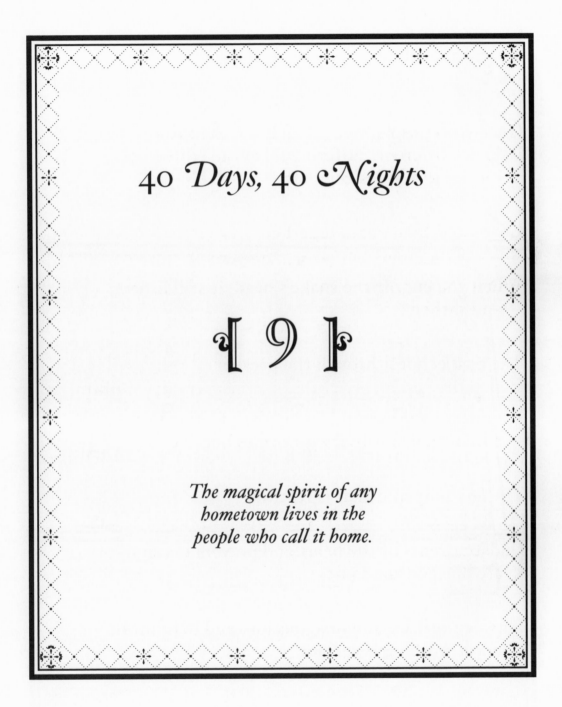

40 Days, 40 Nights

{ 9 }

The magical spirit of any hometown lives in the people who call it home.

*W*ho will save us from ourselves?

Once someone survives cataclysm, the future
    looks different; suffering takes on a different
    meaning, as does laughter.

Chaos and calm come together.

When you cut off the snake's head, it still bites
    and slithers.

The past echoes through the present.

We temper the turmoil and make a pact with the
    pain inside, but it always comes back.

The anatomy of deceit is fetching.

Undercurrents of the heart and prayers in purgatory
    are one and the same.

Between realism and imagination, and behind the
    mask, nothing is certain.

The mind believes what lies next to the heart.

Family skeletons that cannot be buried must be
made to sing and dance.

What is risky is exciting.

The voice of dissent is a dangerous thing not to use.

Fate has a crooked finger.

When the past and present collide, dense layers of
meaning emerge.

Danger lurks everywhere.

Behind public façade invariably there is a private soul.

We are all courtesans, at one time or another.

Some contours of sadness are unapproachable,
bottomless.

Narrow minds travel narrow roads.

There is wisdom in our burdens and deep despair.

Oblivion has a certain appeal, and allure.

To argue with the fates is useless and pointless;
    they get their way without compromise.

Wrestling with antagonists strengthens and
    sharpens our resolve.

It is never a bad idea to delay misery.

The face paints portraiture of the mind; the eyes
    are its scouts.

Spider webs united can even snare a lion.

The life of man is a spectacle, a circus, with a
    nearby ringmaster.

Do not mistake disenchantment for truth.

Calamity and tragedy call forth and unveil heroes
    and cowards.

Everyone has nameless needs.

When we look back, we see ourselves wafting
    across the silver screen, our entire existence but
    a grainy, late-night movie blurred into a dream
    or maybe a nightmare.

One who knows most believes least.

The entire world can be seen with clarity from the
    seat of a Ferris wheel.

Both winners and losers fall down.

It is good to be suspicious of suspicious minds.

The fine art of gossip is an ancient pastime,
    with the pain inflicted more lasting and lethal
    than any bayonet.

Dark shadows cover and conceal many things.

The hideous is fascinating.

Family trees can have rotten roots.

When we awake from sleep, crisis shows us
　　whether we have grown strong or weak.

Petty fights are the most dangerous.

Beelzebub can come clothed as one of the cool,
　　beautiful people.

It is far better to live rich than to die rich.

Hardships make us humble, yet fiery and brave.

In the dark we dance in Dante's Inferno.

A grief shared begins to find some semblance
　　of peace.

We have to live with the choices we make.

There is no evil without good, no good without evil.

Piety does not pay.

All things despised fragment and fall apart,
　　sooner or later.

Dare to be defiant.

To trot out the past and examine it in great detail
does nothing to vanquish or quiet the pain that
lies there.

Never trust your heart to a carnivore.

Settled angers, hibernating in the heart, often
rekindle from the embers.

Fate is capricious, mysterious and unjust.

Improbable people make interesting friends.

The days of adversity make the fleeting feel of
prosperity far more joyful.

Life is a parody.

A heart of duplicity is deceitful and wicked above
all things.

The face of hell is molded from truths recognized
too late.

All sanctuaries have a price.

Emperors rarely appear as ferocious and foreboding
in their nakedness.

Man is a maker of martyrdom and gods.

Trust instinct to the end, when the choice is to
ignore logic and disregard reason.

Many smiles hide a taste for blood.

To be jealous of beauty, makes you ugly.

Both golden shackles and iron shackles can confine
and suffocate the soul.

Disciples can be dangerous.

The memory recalls haunting echoes of the
reverberating footsteps not taken, down the
corridor to the door not taken, leading to the
gateway not opened; we hush our muffled regrets.

People sometimes hear what we do not say.

The most deadly of all passions is a lust for power.

We often try to follow hollow footprints in the dust.

Though the body and heart suffer a great anguish,
    the spirit may profit. So they say.

We build our own pine boxes, whether they be
    plain or jewel encrusted.

To survive it is sometimes necessary to fight, and
    those who fight must be unafraid of getting
    dirty and bloodied.

He who toils with pain will embrace pleasure all
    the more.

The cloak of concealment nourishes vice.

A sliver of the soul of those whom we have loved
    seeps into us, clings to us, and we carry it
    everywhere we go.

We are prisoners of our own attachments.

The tongue is a wild beast to let loose, yet difficult
to chain.

Fear and dread fill the mouth often, suffocating us.

The procession of the past interrupts and punctuates
the present.

Few ever do find what they are looking for.

Sanity is most often held together by a single thread.

We speed toward the dark night of the soul, hurling
toward the naked truth.

The Sphinx holds answers to many riddles.

Regret over yesterday and fear of tomorrow can
drive us mad.

The winds of sadness blow through every life.

Many go up and come down the stairway to hell.

The blackness within devours us.

Look for the shadows and footprints of a serpent.

Out of the darkness comes many answers.

Cold marble slabs speak their own romantic text,
    with echoes of the vanishing light.

The light sheds darkness.

Who does not crave to capture and hold on to a
    moment already passed?

The alcove of the heart is a deadly place.

A memoir of fate and the unfolding of what
    remains is rarely sweetly written.

The thrill of touching a memory lives on over time.

Have the courage to make a fool of yourself.

Apologies are seeped in musty traces of what went
    before, never to be totally blotted out.

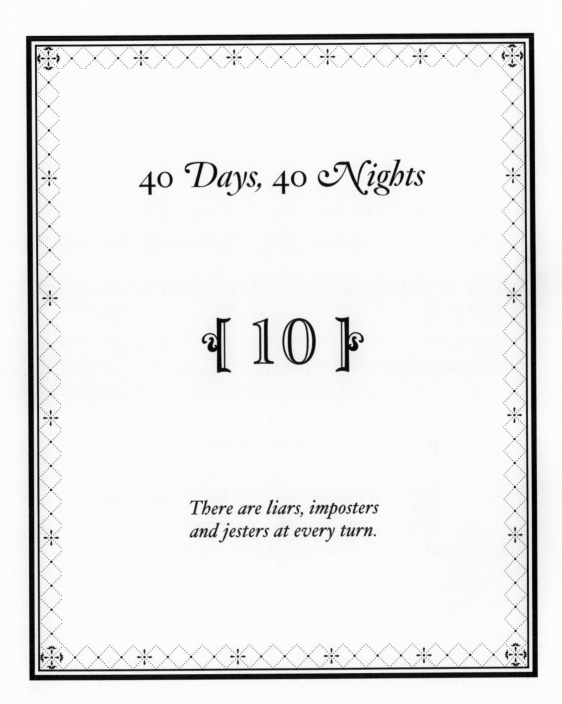

40 *Days,* 40 *Nights*

{ 10 }

*There are liars, imposters
and jesters at every turn.*

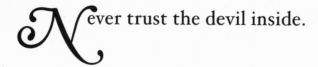ever trust the devil inside.

Quirks, dreams and contrivances serve to shape
who we are.

There lives a tableau in the mind, of secrets and
things unsaid.

A battered and damaged soul is better than no
soul at all.

Find your own moral compass.

The passion of rage and revenge leads to quiet
conspiracy in the shadows.

Valor, decency and hell often come wrapped as one.

Tragedy and transformation go hand-in-hand.

Everyone has shadows on the soul.

Passion is required to hurl into the
continental unknown.

Satyrs have seductive smiles.

A lethal blend of anger and melancholy, twists
us inside.

Do not always slay the anger inside, as it sometimes
serves to come forth.

Empires fall.

An army of darkness lives inside our heads, invading
our thoughts.

Racing along the road of life, many parts are left
behind, severed along the highway, never to be
found or reclaimed.

Fate is unavoidable.

You are not imagining it, there is always something
coming after you.

Paranoid people are often right.

Resist being scolded and molded.

The necklace of the world rests heavily upon
the shoulders.

Power brings pleasure and pain.

Usually, there are few road signs and guideposts to
take you to the place where you are going.

The right path is not always paved.

Conflict and controversy stir the world, igniting
the senses.

Mistakes can be right.

The further you step from the person you want to
be, the harder it is to return.

Justice is subjective and subversive.

The heart seeks to know and understand what it
cannot comprehend.

Many voices cry in the wasteland.

Apparitions of who and what we were haunt us.

The gods play chess, checkers and checkmate with
    our lives.

Winged lions fly free.

Most winners in life feel like failures inside, that is
    what drives, propels and pushes them on. But it is
    better to be a failure who feels like a winner inside.

We leave behind scattered pieces of our soul, as we go.

Many whispers come at midnight.

Nobody knows another person's world, not really,
    not ever.

When in doubt, trust the gut more than the brain.

The horizon and the abyss are both close at hand.

Everything possesses perishability.

In a blink, values melt, puddle and float away.

It is okay to rail against life's cruel disappointments
and diabolical humiliations.

Quirky is good.

There is a dark underbelly caveat to most things
good, including people.

Most truths are hidden.

The other side of open doors can lead to new
understanding.

We make our own cages.

It is good to acquire a sense of fearlessness; or at
least to fake it.

Fate and mere mortals have a tricky relationship.

It is good to be possessed, by something.

What burns brightly in the soul cannot be snuffed out.

There is no sanctity or redemption in hypocrisy.

Life relies upon the flip of a coin.

The reek and breath of repose are never welcome.

Cloud nine comes to rest directly above purgatory.

Fond illusion and frequent self-delusion are among
    life's most magical elixirs.

One life leads to another. So we hope.

There are many rooms, mansions, hearts and
    minds of individual suffering.

It is difficult to harness and shout down the winds
    of change.

Uncharted territory is the most rewarding.

The heart is the story of your life, of your lives,
    loves and losses, of traces of the past, vestiges of
    memories and the passage of time.

Portraits of majesty are intoxicating; mottled
    deceit hides veiled illusion.

Life revolving, ebbing and flowing, outlives catastrophe.

The sun, moon and stars shall have their say; in the
end they prevail.

Well-behaved people seldom make history.

A dissent into madness sometimes brings emergence,
on the other side.

Fragments of a slivered soul hide many secrets.

Imposters are usually unmasked in the end.

The luxurious qualities of youth, a lavish life and
the fine things that go with a borrowed
existence, soon dissipate.

It is never smart to defy the gods.

Beware of embracing a flame-eyed devil in disguise.

Evil has many masks, many charms, many poisons.

To tempt fate is to be scorched by it.

Cherished and shadowy memories hold many
    secret stories known only to thyself.

The devil never presents himself as Satan with a
    pitchfork and bifurcated tail.

Our memories precede us.

Death is closing in on us, every minute; it surrounds us.

Many seemingly sweet souls are actually driven by
    demons and mangled minds.

When we swallow our sorrows for too long we
    strangle on silent sobs.

Trust breeds deceit.

When all the road signs of your former life vanish,
    where do the heartbroken go? How do they ever
    find their way home again?

You can never forget what you have seen.

Life leads us to many paths with the same truths.

The hunt always looks different in the eyes of the
   hunted than in the eyes of the hunter.

We all race through the maze trying to beat death —
   seeking to outrun, outpace, outsmart it — however,
   the last laugh is on us as eventually we turn the
   corner, somewhere, sometime, someplace, and
   there is death, staring us straight in the face.

It is easy to fall into the sky.

Many beautiful people, tanned by perpetual
   sunshine and idleness, dwell peacefully
   in their whipped-cream cities, seeing the good
   life through amber-colored glasses.

It is by going deep down into the abyss that we
   recover the treasures of life.

Grief has its own agenda.

Not all martyrs survive the wretched pits of
   pandemonium.

It is impossible to bar the thief of time from entering.

The past traipses through our head, rewriting history.

We have an inborn tendency to cling to a hope, a
dream and a belief in something beyond human
reach or understanding.

The stranger in the mirror is the most dangerous
enemy of all.

Who can resist challenging the good judgment and
moral authority of lesser gods?

It is best to live life on the edge.

There is promise and peril in the dream unraveling.

Faded memories take their own special toll.

No one can tell you how to grieve and when to stop.

Everyone loves a brilliant and irreverent rake.

Dissenters are often silenced.

40 Days, 40 Nights

{ 11 }

The face in the window
never goes away.

Our paradise is our prison.

When the moment we seek to capture has come and
gone, we are but ghosts of our former selves.

Those who run from fate collide with it sooner
or later.

No one can avoid being stripped of illusion and
tossed into the abyss.

The world is full of shattered perceptions; we toast
and torture ourselves with the shards.

Never fall victim to believing your own lies.

The mirror reflects the false front of a flawed person.

Serpents whisper with devil's breath.

Voices that have disappeared into the dust still call
out to us.

Some hells are unlike any other.

Flying too close to the sun can cremate the soul.

To repent is to waste wanton time.

Riches give the illusion of intelligence.

Life is a spiraling circle of pleasure and pain,
    ecstasy and agony.

Dreams can bring deception.

Sometimes our hearts break open so wide we seem
    to travel out to the stars and beyond, until it is
    no longer beating in our chest.

Push the boundaries.

The end is where we began.

Shouts, whispers and murmurs change the world.

The heart is an unfaithful shrine.

We all descend into a dark pit of pain; there is no
    painless passage.

The years can make you bitter.

It is not uncommon to have prolonged encounters
   with the darkness, whether these be obvious or
   hidden.

The journey is the destination, to somewhere.

Human beings see through a dark prism of illusion.

Secrets underpin passions.

The sun and shadow, the light and dark, forever
   alternate deep within our souls.

Where there is good, there must be bad.

The only true path to remembering wisdom is by
   way of suffering.

What cannot be cured must be endured.

The nefarious night of the soul strips us bare,
   creating new awakenings, new beginnings.

It is an epic voyage to the bottom.

Mankind and history are illogical, unjust and chaotic.

A fool lives poor to die rich.

What does not seduce you, makes you weaker.

There is no good or evil in the world; it is only
where you stand on the seesaw of life.

Reality is fleeting, but illusion prevails.

Both the sinner and saint sometimes dance with
the devil.

Life is random.

Nothing can keep you safe from the pain nor dry
from the rain.

Rarely is one mistake fatal in itself.

Infinite tears are counted and heard by somebody,
somewhere, sometime.

There is black in white, white in black.

Money makes men mad.

Grief is fluid, it never goes away, never heals; it just
ebbs and flows with the tides of life, changing
shape and form.

Love and hate are liquid fire personified.

All things temporal melt, evaporate and slip from
our lives.

What is done in the dark comes to light.

To be fully alive and not just sleepwalking we need to
feel the hot breath of death and danger somewhere
nearby, breathing hard down our neck, chilling our
soul, closing in fast.

Extreme sanity is highly overrated.

Dancing as fast as we can, we run in circles along
the slippery slope of the bottomless pit.

This world is fractured.

It is impossible to see who conceals broken jagged
    glass inside.

Failures lead to greatness.

Some of the jokes life plays on a person border on
    being downright sadistic.

Who the gods love die young.

In times of trouble laugh like a hyena. Sometimes
    it helps.

Evil waits like a parasite to invade the soul.

Upstairs and downstairs, there is fire in heaven
    and hell.

In time, you will have pain.

The hot breath of eternity blows on our backs,
    bearing down on our necks.

Small sticks cast big shadows.

Being safe and secure is a fool's illusion, a figment
of our imaginations.

What we imagine, we manifest.

There are shadows that we do not see above us
and behind us, invisible faces, burning bright in
the nightglow.

Everyone's life is a dark jewel of a story.

You have to accept heartache, feel it and embrace it;
there is no way to avoid it, nowhere to hide, or run.

Depravity knows no boundaries.

Visions in the rearview mirror always appear clearer
than in the windshield.

No one can outrun time.

Even heroes have the right to bleed, cry and fail.

In time, memories fade and melt into untruths.

The world is an infinite sphere that we — with innocence and oblivion — pace back-and-forth upon the dissolving surface of.

Reason does not rule the world.

Demons can be controlled and tamed, but only temporarily.

What lurks beneath is always there, near or far, close by, somewhere.

Nobody understands this life, not really.

The sun, moon and stars are never as pretty up close.

Some people have nothing behind the eyes.

To hell and back is a journey rarely completed.

Step back when peering into hell.

The frostbite of sadness cannot be warmed.

Marshmallowy clouds are not nearly as soft or
    clean as they look.

Danger intoxicates the soul.

A fine line runs between those we love to hate and
    those we hate to love.

Wickedness of mind, selfishness of character, and
    will to power are sometimes masked by beauty
    and nobility.

Blessings and curses are one and the same.

We kill ourselves from the inside out.

Control of things in life, control of any sort, always
    does inevitably slip, slip away.

There is only one law in the universe that never
    changes; that is, all things change, and all things
    are impermanent. Nothing endures but change.

Schemes work.

Friends, family and lovers sometimes draw us into
the warm, safe white light, for a time, at least;
yet we are forever pulled back, down and under
by the bottomless current that flows and rages
deep inside, seeking to return us into the
destructive darkness from which we came, that
which we know best.

The truth is transient.

Anti-heroes are heroes to many.

We move intrepidly through life by revisiting
scenes of bygone days, whether those visions are
factual or fond illusion.

Out of the past comes a portrait of the future.

Macabre tales contain sparkles of gauzy wisdom.

We make our own persnickety, pious prisons.

Glossy, venomous-looking people attract us.

40 Days, 40 Nights

{ 12 }

Whispers of yesterday
foretell of tomorrow.

*L*ove first, live fortuitously.

Many temples, shrines, churches, palaces and
walls line the prettily paved gateway to glory,
ruin and Babylon.

Calamity invariably leaves a large handprint on
tomorrow.

Descending and ascending from the mirage of a
vertical horizon, an ominous black overcast of
collapse and crisis can suddenly ride in as a devil
plunderer in the night, rampaging all we love.

A fatal flaw is rarely obvious.

Whatever you are, you do not always have to be.

Images that touch prove tough to dislodge, offering
a tantalizing window into our own soul.

The heart illuminates the way to heaven or hell.

We fall victim to red lipstick and evil machines.

What captures our mind's eye molds and shapes
the outcome of our days and nights.

Time past is always tinted and rouged, stained
and washed.

Misery, mistakes and regrets bog us down for
too long.

What passes for reality can be denied.

Enduring emblems of the lockstep of man and
time are strangely comforting to us.

Let life wrap around and envelop you.

The sands of time shift, reviewed over the shoulder,
drift and alter shape, forever restless.

We are all heroes and villains.

All life is filled with danger, loss, survival, courage
and endurance.

Chaos is never tamed.

One day your stories and memories will be gone, too.

Most people are neither well or ill, just unwell.

Life is a one-way ticket, an unchartered voyage
    with no return passage.

Seemingly inconsequential things create deadly
    enemies and wars.

In the end, the gaze of death equalizes all.

Most see the surface of life without ever
    understanding the depth.

It is okay to ruffle feathers with one's views.

Nothing stays the same forever. And sometimes
    not for a day.

There is a place beyond emotion and desire.

We all have a history we never tell anyone about.

Memories cannot be easily jettisoned or abandoned.

Shadows lie within shadows.

Life is lashed together with a slipknot. Unstable.
    Extemporaneous.

The unlit side is the more intriguing side.

We all wear many masks, many disguises.

The jagged edges of profound loss, heartache, grief
    and a weathered heart are softened with a shared
    sense of loss.

Life is made up of many stories, moments lost
    and found.

It is not unreasonable to wrap yourself in a covering
    of armor.

Time cannot be bought, nor stopped.

Do not be afraid.

The remaining objects of a life left behind are
    never pretty.

The world is not fair and never will be, but we are not absolved of our obligations to try to reach out and make a difference.

Now is the moment you have been waiting for.

There are many worlds within ourselves.

All that we love, hate and fear is but a complex mirror of our troubles.

The world conspires to consume and wreak havoc on itself.

Silver linings contain clouds.

We have our doubts, but happiness resides in the smudgy shadows of sorrow.

It is often best to take the road not taken.

There is no real equality or deliverance in life, except in death.

Characters thronged in crises are the most memorable.

The devil is rarely as black as he is painted.

We can never forget what we have known and seen,
    the people, places and things that are no more.

Sooner or later, it is over.

It is better to be happy here and now, regardless
    of the circumstances, because there is always
    the invisible threat of — what if tomorrow
    never comes?

Evil follows good, good follows evil.

The most extreme sojourns in life occur in the
    secret chambers of the heart.

Enchantment depends on perception.

We must explore life, quarrel with it, and once in a
    while find the part of it we love.

In dark times, the eyes begin to see.

We are all colored and corroded by our life experiences.

The grave is a lifelong foil.

Some bonds are deep attachments that cannot be broken; sometimes, the past does not let go.

All life is a dream, an illusion.

Tomorrow is an unfinished tale of dreams and stories yet to be told.

Idyll does not last.

We traverse life by retracing the timeworn grooves of others.

Humor is a good defense.

There is no everlasting season in the sun, no door where an obituary wreath has not hung.

Many roads lead from nowhere to nothing.

We all have a running dialogue with our own history.

Crusaders find and command their audience.

Time immemorial indents and defines our present,
 foreshadowing the future.

No one commands an exclusive claim on the
 unholy mess and ramifications of disaster.

The boundaries between fact and fiction are porous.

We can never be what we were.

All life is but a memory, except for the razor-edge
 twilight of each fleeting moment.

The years roll on, no matter.

What the world has brought together cannot
 be erased.

Live life with intensity.

Those unable to feel deep sorrow can never feel
 deep joy.

Power corrupts, absolutely.

Widely accepted definitions and terms of conduct
do not always make sense.

The aftermath of life brings ever-present shadows
lurking near at hand.

We all swim in a sea of anarchy.

There is no shelter from great sorrow, only a
brief reprieve.

Eventually it is inevitable that you will lick and
taste the flames of a hades.

Naturally beautiful people are accidents of nature.

Time is the currency that really counts.

We are drawn to embrace a certain amount of pain,
evil and danger.

Life is filled with precariousness and collapse, with
the splattering of pretense colored in with tiny
increments of normalcy.

Life and death live side-by-side.

Power moves in a circle.

All we have known and loved stays with us always,
   alive and well and dancing in our mind's eye; we
   shall never say farewell even if we never again
   are graced with the opportunity to cast eyes
   upon all we have known and loved.

There is actuality in myths.

We are capable of more than we learned or imagined.

Life is a series of chapters, a continuum.

All fear is bondage.

No one knows exactly how far away are heaven
   and hell.

To change the future, you must change the past.

40 Days, 40 Nights

{ 13 }

*Everyone seeks love and
redemption before the graveyard.*

We are never out of harm's way.

The essence of life is a constant reinvention, as nothing stays the same for long.

We are our own savior and destroyer.

If you look close enough, you will see rot just beneath the surface.

Wishing upon a star can bring forth poison, fairytales and prophets.

Be as crazy as your conscience allows.

Many buy into the lie that there is safety in objects.

Life is a portrait of dalliances in purgatory.

Postcards from perdition trail the tail of a serpent.

There is a divine power within.

Laugh along; then, if appropriate, strike back.

Most everyone's story is heavy, full of pain, woe
   and loss.

Live and do as you want.

The blackbird of misfortune can lead you to
   migrate to a new path.

We all stand on the edge, the ledge between life
   and death.

In life, run fast; run as long and hard as you can
   since the landscape is littered with corpses and
   coffins, a scenario from which there is no escape.

The more law, the less justice.

Many enemies are relentless and insatiable.

The fires of passion invite us all to get warmed, then
   burned and ravished, by the devouring heat.

Wisdom and foolishness are nearly the same.

There is power, peril and promise in passion.

Somewhere along the serpentine circle of a twisty
   life, there is always the beginning of the end.

We are our own worst tormentors.

Some prefer to pay no heed to unbearably blue skies.

The turning universe is pierced with thunder,
   suspicions and sadness.

We all live in limbo.

Embossed deep into the brain are the things we
   can never figure out.

That which is soothing can also be treacherous.

Insanity and passion are closely linked.

Fate leads us to go down one last time into the flames.

Happily-ever-after always frays at the edges.

The siren's wail beckons us onto the rocks, and
   over the edge.

Money and fame can dissolve into a trainwreck of
    booze and mental illness.

Poison runs in the family veins.

It is better to face the demons than to turn your
    back on them.

Paper roses look real at first, like imitation love.

No one can avoid fear: fear of being alone, of
    being rejected, of being abandoned, of not being
    good enough.

Run with your spirit.

The opposite of love is not hate but fear.

Sometimes the natural order of the world dissolves
    and chaos reigns supreme.

At your mother's death, another one will not come.

Terror and pathos go hand-in-hand.

A great deal of good comes from confronting
   our fears.

Evil, horror, darkness and chaos balance the good,
   goodness, divine and light. One side cannot
   exist without the other.

Much in life does not make sense using reason
   and logic.

There is no remedy or healing for hidden grief.

A frenzy can clear the head.

Those who claim to know everything have the
   most to unlearn.

Do not surrender easily to Armageddon.

Joy is often guarded by the gates of grief.

Some things and persons can never be tamed
   nor possessed.

Eminent disaster hangs heavy in the air.

The mask of a face can conceal the dead, dry poison
hidden behind the falsely glittering eyes.

Danger is rooted in malaise.

We are the architect and interior designer of our
own misery.

The hands of Father Time are so very cruel.

It is good to operate outside the constraints of
normal convention.

Life will maim you.

Tragedy plus the passage of time equals comedy.

All ghosts are hungry.

The only universal truths are those crass and crude
enough to be thought so.

Live fast and dangerously, as often as possible.

Bitter bruises buried deep are sometimes hard to see.

The closed door often obscures the open door.

Pathos and pathology make heroes and villains
   interesting.

Be comfortable with controversy.

Remembrances of things past set demons dancing
   in one's head.

The gods roll the dice.

Who pulls the strings of life's dreadful masquerade ball?

It is sometimes good to savor the poetry of revolt,
   and menace.

There is evidence of things unseen.

One must head into the great unknown to find the
   holy grail.

The worst demons are the unseen and imagined
   ones that hold us prisoner.

Some problems run too deep to be fixed.

Trampling on somebody's turf is the best way
    to get ahead.

Hellish ranting and raving can be good salvo
    for the soul.

It is sometimes good to embark on treacherous paths.

There is no ordinary life.

Many live in a sleepwalk daze, smiling and nodding,
    walled up in a dark prison cell of rage and grief.

Trauma tears up the ethical rulebook.

A maze leads us to the house of many mansions.

Tragedies reveal things about our world and ourselves
    that otherwise stay comfortably hidden.

Do not let the fire in your soul flicker out.

The saviors are us.

There is always a hidden trapdoor into which one
could fall at any given moment.

Everyone needs more than one life to live.

The best way to get where you are going, is to
go too far.

It is good to be a warrior-poet.

Out of desperation comes something you thought
you could never do.

Fabled beauty fades away.

The slings and arrows of misfortune are often
self-inflicted.

What maims you, makes you stronger.

Those who have nothing to lose are willing to
risk everything.

Promises made should be kept.

Nobody knows what lives in your dreams in darkness.

The passage of time scrambles all.

Only madmen and saints willingly jump into the
fire and abyss.

Life is a battleground of good and evil.

We all grapple with the weight of our own debts
and burdens, whether they be real or imagined.

All long to reach into the past and recapture what
was, what is already vanished.

Life — insistent, unyielding, unstoppable — comes
crashing, seeping onto us from all angles and
corners, assaulting our senses and sensibilities.

People delight in a whiff of impropriety.

Stay alive, as long as possible.

40 Days, 40 Nights

{ 14 }

*Most journeys have no
beginning, no end.*

$\mathcal{B}$e a peacock among wrens.

To walk through a wall of fear and unholy baptisms
takes eyes closed, not wide open.

Wild angels are far more enthralling than tame devils.

Pretty, silken little witches are the most dangerous.

The mosaic of life is a maze, a puzzle, with interlocking
pieces alternatively magical and monstrous.

Life can take us on a headlong dive into degradation.

The face is the mask, mirror and window into thy self.

Do not surrender to tomorrow today.

Unspoken words explode like dynamite in the throat.

Even an ape can see an apostle in the mirror.

Happiness is unexplainable and indefinable.

A challenge is always a threat.

Sometimes we step onto a road, a path that we
are meant to be on and from which there is no
turning back.

Pain causes introspection.

We live in a three-level mirage at once — the
future is part of the present and past, and the
past always affects the present and future.

Refuse to play by the rules.

Short-term salvation is seldom worth the price.

At times, life seems surreal, like the world is
spinning in slow motion, magnified.

Never be afraid to flout convention.

Free birds with unclipped wings often fly too high
and fast, soon losing their way before fast-falling
to earth.

Time reduces all in its path to rubble.

A thousand lies make you older.

Some words that fill our ears shred the soul,
    tearing our insides to pieces so that we retreat
    into our solitude.

We connive our own humiliations.

Sensibilities should be untamed.

When the gods punish and mock us, they answer
    our pleas.

Nobody lives a life free from sorrow, regret and
    harrowing loss; we must bleed and grieve — that
    is the human condition.

Salvation is never near.

In the winter of discontent we search for small
    scraps of joy and silence of the soul.

Obstacles always lie ahead.

The world has many golden prisoners trapped in
houses of lies.

Encircling black buzzards wait on the horizon.

The cold and crooked hands of fate are cruel
and calloused.

All things fade away.

Tonnages of gold bring heavier shackles than a
gilded coffin destroying all.

Disaffected people have hearts of darkness.

The pursuits that consume us inevitably destroy us.

Foolhardy romantics can become deranged.

Life is a dark, glittering portrait of unsettled
shadows and debts.

To go deep is to risk drowning.

If you cannot join them, beat them.

Why is what is supposed to be undesirable often
    irresistible?

The Garden of Eden and Sodom and Gomorrah are
    really the same place, the exact same destination
    in disguise, because pleasure breeds peril in the
    same way that ecstasy and agony come paired
    together as weirdly evil twins, as if one begets
    the other and vice versa.

Some are born different, and defiant, with a
    bruised heart, a boulder on the shoulder.

The years have no seasons, for those who are
    mobile, ubiquitous, free.

When desperation claws at the heart, anything
    can happen.

Shadows of sadness lurk behind the eyes.

Many are defiant, hungry for love, for danger, for
    fairytales, too; and therein lies the root of many
    ruinations, inevitably, a meteoric rise and
    descent into heaven and hell on earth.

No one wants to puncture myths.

Strangled minds become threaded with poisonous
sheets of hate.

Refuge can come in unexpected places.

Like an eternal malignant shadow, some of us have
incurable and inoperable fatal flaws.

There lives a den of darkness inside.

He who wins the rat race is still a rat.

We have to hemorrhage, in life, and be burned to the
bone, repeatedly, to know that we are really alive.

Emotional fireworks prove you are really alive.

It is not uncommon to have a thirst for danger and
dangerous liaisons.

There is always a last train to paradise, which
everyone wishes to ride.

One little misstep can seal your fate, forever,
    altering it for all of eternity.

The worst kind of hell is a slow hell.

People with deep, dark troubles always do like liquor.

Certainties are false and fickle.

Murphy's Law always prevails, because it is the
    highest law in the land.

Searing love burns itself into the soul.

When the sun sets, the night is like a menacing
    animal, unpredictable, predatory, and ready
    to pounce.

To mourn anew helps us heal.

People with small minds usually have large prejudices.

See the enemy inside.

The truth is carnal.

When we step through the wall of oblivion we
   reemerge a different person.

A bruised and battered heart is the most defiant.

We often run from our destiny, only to be snared.

It is abnormal to be normal.

We journey in this world lost and lonely, emptiness
   draining our life, drowning in darkness.

The finger of destiny can move quickly or slowly,
   hastening or delaying our torture.

We all dice with the edge of madness.

Jealousy takes people to ruin.

So many precious words, thoughts and feelings,
   buried deep down inside, suddenly slip from the
   mouth and soul, evaporating and scattering to
   the four winds, never to be found again.

Nobody is a football captain forever.

When the curtain falls, forever, there is nothing
    left except the echoes of a life lived.

Everyone has beauty and ugliness.

Fear still triggers fight or flight.

The poorer one is the more devils they meet; but
    the rich fall, too.

Chaos rules supreme.

We are rarely forewarned of the triumph and
    ultimate tragedy of flying too near the sun.

The gifts that evil brings, evil also takes away.

Ice water and lava can pour from the eyes as tears.

The truth can be like a dank, dark, cold vault.

Striking evil in human form rarely reveals its true
    colors, until it is too late.

The tragic and the comic intersect.

Without hope and illusion what would we have,
other than ashes and emptiness?

Sometimes camouflage is necessary.

The devils inside only remain chained up for so
long, before breaking loose.

In the bleakest of days, disillusionment is sometimes
followed by a reawakening as we respond to life's
overwhelming challenges.

Perfection is bland and characterless.

The lure of fractured people and places is
always seductive.

Everything, everyone, everywhere — it all ends.

Approach life with irreverence.

The unresolved past always lurks nearby in exile.

40 Days, 40 Nights

{ 15 }

*All houses of brick and mortar
are built on sand and fog.*

What you chase, rarely sets you free.

Be careful for whom you decide to strip your soul bare.

A man who trusts no one is untrustworthy.

When we stare at the sad remnants, the final vestiges
of a life lost, we are forever changed.

An overexamined life leads nowhere.

Cool, calm and collected people often conceal a
disturbed state of mind.

We rarely know when death's vague taste and
obscure smell is so very close at hand.

Being good is a trap.

Tomorrow is promised to no one, not to the
rainmaker, to the archangels, nor to the man
who sells his soul to gain the universe.

We all search for answers that answer nothing.

Raw edges and shimmering fantasies are usually
   well hidden.

Never ignore the ramblings of a madman. What if
   they are the truth?

A perfect moment can suddenly seesaw into
   something dark and contorted.

Soak up the languor while you can.

The creative mind is a fragmented jigsaw puzzle,
   with important pieces missing.

Do not turn away from what you feel.

When we are grateful for our blessings and thank
   our lucky stars that they simply snigger at us,
   they already know what is really in store.

Nice people get pulverized.

Uncanny whispers of foreboding sometimes dance
   in our head, as a chill of warning flicks across
   our spine — all of which we generally ignore.

All men want to be rich.

We all search for that mythical place, somewhere over
the rainbow, where dreams actually do come true:
fool's paradise, the roadmap to hell.

Death is the great leveler.

Most all of life, beauty and youth included, is simply
borrowed and not ours to keep for long.

Wrath is steely and long-lived.

It does not pay to be too nice; antics and
misbehavior are often far more effective.

Dare to be different.

No matter how gallantly we fence with time, we
lose the duel.

There are many heavens, many hells.

We like to hold tight to people who are a little
bit dangerous.

The past controls the present.

Life is lived in a sunny pit of sweet madness and
glorious sadness, side-by-side with a river of
thieves and vultures that barricade the way.

Never go quickly or softly into the night.

One who digs too deep should be prepared
for the buried remains they unearth, often
still smoldering.

What is phantom can seem so real.

Any small comfort you might find will be transient
and temporary.

Masks conceal many secrets.

Peace and forgiveness are generally fleeting.

The hurricane inside continues to turn and churn.

When possible, buy now, pay later.

Humans pine for what is lost, what can never be again.

Not to know is to know.

Mortals who dare to claim the power and perfection
of the gods get maimed and scorched.

The vanishing point is not so far.

A constant quest for perfection and a mistake-free
life sabotage any chance of happiness.

Your vice can be your virtue.

The threads of our relationships weave the tapestry
of our lives, hopes, dreams and fears.

Wisdom does not produce courage.

Some mistakes can be unwoven or rewoven; others
forever remain embedded into the fabric of our life.

We dance and flit our way across the stage of life,
oblivious to what lies ahead just across the chasm.

Ice sometimes covers the fire beneath.

We are prisoners of the vaults and tombs of our
   own making.

The past torments.

And the sad music of darkness plays on and on.

The sky falls in on top of us, suffocating us.

We are seduced and solicited to heaven or hell,
   sooner or later.

To be lost, is to be found.

Outcasts live the freest, most unfettered of lives.

The greater the knowledge, the greater the sorrow.

It is best to never look back to see how far we have
   come, or not.

The conspiracy of sanctity, hypocrisy and prophecy
   often go together.

Anger mismanagement sometimes works well.

Everything the power of the world does is done
    in a circle.

A fair-weather friend is no better than a foe.

It is difficult for a devil to see himself.

We are often homesick for places and precious
    moments that we have never known, a past that
    will not let go.

Illusion is always stronger than reality.

Sometimes we long to disappear into nothingness.

There is no courage without fear.

When dark furies are set loose on us, there is
    nowhere to hide.

Humankind continues to toil and dream against
    all odds.

Painful things stalk and torture us on earth.

The world is a perilous landscape, and as we
    hopscotch our way through the treacherous
    minefield of life — with optimism and hope
    leading us on, with a narrow margin for error —
    it is true, our existence hangs in perpetual limbo
    because we never know what is in store for us
    around the next corner.

Hope in the heart enables denial in the brain.

The green-eyed dragon of jealousy knows no
    boundaries.

Our own perspiration strangles us.

We often stand poised in front of the porthole to
    hell without knowing it.

The grim reaper camps upon our doorstep.

We live life by making giant leaps of faith.

Howling skeletons race behind us, closing in fast.

Rip through the layers of deceit without regret.

Those who hold onto courage can conquer much.

Who will heal the healers?

Secrets are best cloaked in damp darkness.

We must honor and remember what we see transpire.

Adversaries savor scandal and the revelation of dark
    secrets; but the strong are unafraid to cross swords.

That which chills can also thrill.

Actuality is an illusion and nothing is as it seems, ever.

Hell and heaven on earth fuse together.

Passion smashes through all barriers to hold you
    hostage on the ride of your life, sometimes
    taking you to a point of no return.

We all dangle at death's door.

The merciless, unyielding flow of time, restless and
    relentless, shifts and drifts upon this temporal
    world, altering the shape of everything we value.

Fairness and unfairness are doled out in
    uneven measure.

Lost in the walls of our memory are trapped
    embers of time, ashes caught in shadows,
    helping to heal despair and soften sorrows as we
    live in the afterglow.

A liar lies to himself.

Not all reveal a bottomless well of sadness,
    bitterness and guilt.

Suspension of disbelief is necessary to survive
    life's riddles.

Bullheadedness can get you through.

In the face of gloom, parade back from the grave's edge.

40 Days, 40 Nights

{ 16 }

Who does not cry for yesterday.

He who runs is followed.

The fascination for ruin is romantic and seductive.

Even heroes crack and crumble.

The voices that come before us lay carved in the
floorboards.

Decline and revival is a cycle.

Porcelain gods are cold and hard; they know nothing
of flesh and blood.

Doomed fairytales intrigue us.

There is nothing like love to cure our ills, soothe
our souls, nothing like love to break our hearts,
scorch our souls.

Who can resist tempting fate?

Silky-soft poison goes down sweetly and does not
smart until much later.

We always see the places where we used to live, the
   people we used to be.

Look inside, for answers.

Flame-eyed hellions come in disguise, love shining
   in their vacant eyes.

Good and evil come as matched twins.

Encrusted colorings of the past coat and varnish
   the portrayal we depict of our lives.

Do not drown in this great vale of tears.

Unseen ancient memories are whispering, sagging
   and heavy, floating through the air.

There is no escape, but escape itself.

No matter where we go, we carry faded pieces of
   the past with us.

The strongest cardinal points of the compass
   are internal.

All the big themes that weave through life contain
    tragedy.

There is parody in pathos.

When you climb too high, there is nowhere left
    to climb.

Memories do not match real life.

When you grab a piece of stardust, run with it.

If you are alive it is unavoidable to not know sorrow
    and loss on a first-name basis.

The night is long and life is short.

Even grand dames covet.

There is no safe harbor or sanctuary. Period.

Life requires a blind jump into the abyss.

Everyone, at some point, is falling backwards in time.

You do not have to be twenty and perfect to have a life.

The most important opinion is your own.

Evil spun in silk like a spider's cache is spellbindingly bewitching.

Answers are reflected in the looking glass.

The church of the poisoned mind is a saintly altar for many.

Only the strong can forgive.

Sometimes we wish our fake life was real, our real life fake.

The future scrawls itself upon our history.

Even though you might be in the hole, be happy; at least you are not in the big hole yet.

Most destruction comes from the inside.

The trail of deceit leads to high and low places.

Unspoken words sometime speak louder than spoken words.

Dragons beget dragons.

To run to the middle of nowhere, as fast as you can, feels good, for a short while.

An old rival never becomes a friend.

The endless pursuit of heaven is highly overrated.

Faith in humanity helps one heal.

The fates will lead those who follow, and drag those who do not.

We do not want others to know us, or to see us, as we are; not really.

All eyes tell a story.

Charismatic people are not necessarily likable, or honorable.

There is no guarantee, no true safety, ever.

Wishful thinking can put you on the wrong road,
    taking you on cryptic journeys, to dangerous places.

Over-politeness is fictitious.

All of us have dark secrets to unearth, dark
    journeys upon which to embark.

It is hard to leave the life we choose.

Provocative is scary and scary is provocative.

What wounds us with a marred scar, makes
    us stronger.

Dark motivation drives people to odd places.

Pain awakens us.

The troubled and deeply conflicted individual is
    good at make believe, at covering up and being
    an ever-so-fabulous fraud.

A secret, silent swamp binds the twisty threads
of life.

Trailblazers move the world forward.

Whether you believe in fate or not, fate is a
weird thing.

An adventurous spirit never grows old.

The devil rides on our coattails; he lives in the
rearview mirror.

We are alone with our angst.

Cold eyes gaze at us from behind hidden clumps
of darkness.

Everyone loves tantalizingly twisted intrigue.

We hurl ourselves closer and closer to the center,
whether we want to or not.

Crazy people are very intelligent.

You are safest in the heart of the lion's den.

Hard conditions ignite the fire of life.

There is nothing worse than dread to fill our
mouths and lungs.

It is easy to get trapped and strangled in a spinning
web of toxic fairytales.

People, places and things that sink low can also
rise to the top.

When luck offers a finger, grab hold of the hand.

No burden is without end.

Those before us, and after us, and those who are
us, are but one in soul and eternity.

Between love and madness lies obsession.

Those who sleepwalk through life end up in the
graveyard sooner than they imagined.

Dishonest people often know how to live well.

The jagged icicles that drip from a frostbitten
heart can be lethal.

Memories are always misty colored.

Follow your heart and the depth of intuition; doors
will open where you did not know they existed.

Self-deception rescues us from ourselves.

Everyone plays games.

The hell-fire-and-brimstone vortex of our hearts
push us to forge ahead, to keep going.

We are prisoners of time and truth.

Try to flee trouble and it will chase you down.

Soulless is the night.

The will to live, to survive, to go on no matter
what, is stronger than you think.

Reality is the ultimate illusion.

If you are safe, happy, loved and protected —
    enjoy it — for it does not last.

Folly brings wisdom.

The charred remains of the day bring no consolation.

People are as an island.

Most ghosts are private ones, undetected and
    hidden behind the eyes of those they haunt.

Even angels of light lie.

Beautiful lies are deeply rooted in ancient truths.

What can flourish from the fallout of Dante's
    Inferno is a Phoenix ascending.

Overbearing people rarely face the music.

40 Days, 40 Nights

{ 17 }

We all choose our own
steeples and holy grails.

*H*onesty is more shocking than dishonesty.

Reckless people who fling themselves through life
with fearless abandon have the most fun.

We all have premonitions of the sacred.

Great love and great achievements require great risk.

Those who do nothing make no mistakes.

Every sepulcher stores unspoken secrets, forever
lost upon the wings of time.

To fall down is to stand tall.

Sometimes we need curtains pulled across our eyes
to block out the light of the world.

Time is a cruel companion.

Untrained demons of the mind run rampant,
refusing to be quieted.

We all feel, I do not belong here.

The netherworld is always nearby.

Grand justice is best served in the hands of
the aggrieved.

Always be prepared for the games to begin.

Time is the soothing salve that heals our pain and
wounds but deceptively steals and snuffs out our
lives, suffocating our heads like a shroud.

Some hurts peel the soul from the bone.

We rarely know when we are in a free-fall swan dive.

The world is fully of mystery, faith, deceit.

People may shed many skins and live many lives.

A wild brain is hardwired to the heart.

Nothing is worse than the thrashing sounds of
anguish and collapse.

The masks of eternity both cover and reveal.

Flinty independence is far better than self-pity.

The passage of time is pain's only ointment.

Holier-than-thou people often take a mighty
     tumble from pious clouds in the sky, landing
     with a dust-devil thud.

That which keeps us safe eventually smothers us.

Deep secrets spawn tall tales.

Some actually do survive, and even thrive on
     Greek tragedies.

Outcasts can go far.

It is possible to scale the gates of hell and survive.

Fame and fortune can be a gilded slavery.

Beauty can belie the beast within.

Castles hung in the sky are the best places to reside.

The monsters are us.

Curse and smash the clocks that bind us to
    time passing.

We all have troubles that cannot be named.

There is no cure; only a temporary transient reprieve.

We are each capable of every wickedness.

The truth is generally an unforgiveably cruel distortion
    of what we know, and believe, to be true.

Deny and defy death as long as possible.

What we run from, what we deny, defy and regret,
    always seems to find and haunt us in the duskiness
    of night, in our dreams.

Arguing with the past does not change it.

The tightrope is best walked with eyes closed.

Everyone wants to possess something, or someone,
   they do not have.

Salvation comes in many disguises.

It is sometimes unwise to turn around and look back.

Swimming against the tide either takes you down
   or makes you stronger.

It is such sweet sorrow that severs the soul.

The mind cannot bear witness to what the heart
   can withstand.

What we see in the head is not there.

Excess on the outside often reveals not enough on
   the inside.

Logic crumbles under the weight of desire.

Many things, both real and imagined, spring to life
   in the shadows.

A life well lived is punctuated with turmoil.

Tormented souls afire light the way and separate a
    path through the wilderness for lesser mortals
    to follow.

We redress ourselves in many cloaks.

Formidable powers of destruction radiate from the
    core of every kinship and friendship.

Nobody lives his dream, not really.

The world laughs and swirls around death and
    dying, oblivious.

Death stares back at us, unblinkingly.

Tigers cannot be tamed.

A deep and thinking mind is an eruption waiting
    to happen.

Many get out of one hell and into another.

The spoken word is soon forgotten, but the written word remains.

Life is like describing mercury; put your finger on it, and it moves.

There is only the now.

Everyone wavers between good and evil.

The loose gravel of life leads to far more interesting places than a cement road.

Few find the abode of the gods.

There is a light in the eclipse that cannot often be seen or found.

Nobody is a star forever.

Reason and logic too rarely yield the right answers.

Mental captivity is the worst prison of all.

Celebutantes taunt but enliven us.

The shadowy demon named death follows and stalks us, yes, everywhere we go; eagerly waiting to swoop down upon us like a big black vulture of a bird with no soul, no conscience.

Your decisions determine your destiny.

Hate kindles hate.

We are all innocent and guilty, predators and prey.

Information does not cure ignorance.

There are worse sins than not being able to recognize the devil when he is knocking on your door.

Hate and admiration are close, sometimes the same.

Chaos and crisis lead to change.

The past is so very far away, the future even further.

Reality depends on perception.

Everyone drinks from the deep cup of irony.

Out of desperation, you find something you think
   you would never do.

Empires fall away, memories remain.

Life is but a psychedelic fantasia, a swirling
   alternating kaleidoscope, of pain and
   pleasure, agony and ecstasy.

Every man is Cain and Abel.

The hand of fate teases and toys with us, brutally
   knocking us down, viciously slapping us around,
   unmercifully so; then it sometimes tenderly
   caresses us, ever so gently, and sweetly. Do not
   be fooled. Be aware. Be vigilant.

Pathos is good.

Mazes and passageways often lead to Babylon's
   inner wall.

Life is a theater of memories, as well as the macabre.

One devil is like another.

Deference and defiance often come packaged as one.

What we fear, we attack or run from.

The mayhem of life oozes menace and misery, in an unreal world of mystery and mercy, magic and make believe.

Drama magnets wield a certain power.

You never know what transpires between two people.

Visible and invisible scars are keepsakes, mementos of the past.

The walls, edges and abysses are indefinable.

We all have devils inside us.

The cinders of time conceal and reveal many riddles.

An unsullied reputation is boring.

40 Days, 40 Nights

{18}

*In the veil of shadows, prying evil eyes
cannot stare a tender soul into oblivion.*

Some cuts are too deep to ever heal.

There is no choice but to dally and dance with
destiny, regardless of the consequences.

What you love can take you down.

That which is dark and destructive often remains
out of sight.

Only myths are immortal.

There is always a war in the head, between dark
and light.

Mystery can bring menace.

A devil's delusions seem so very real, enticing and
bewitching.

Knowledge is not wisdom.

There is pain and yet pleasure in dredging up
dark memories.

There are many ways to artificially feed — but
    never quite fill — that dark, bottomless vat of
    emptiness that lurks deep in the soul.

Everyone must learn how to fall, and fail.

It is impossible to be late for a date with destiny.

Many live in the fast lane of oblivion.

We are capable of much more than we are taught
    to believe.

Confusion and chaos reign supreme.

You cannot have a future unless you have a past,
    and if you are in love with the present then it
    becomes the past, whatever that is.

See the invisible.

When we dance, the sun, moon and stars stand still.

Horror is at the foreground of wonder.

Most people see what they look for, not what is really before them.

Tears are equal part vindication and sorrow.

Pearls of wisdom come at a great price.

In a world of contradictions, the truth lies and lies reveal the truth.

Mere mortals never do get the last laugh.

Cruel false hope is a good thing, but dangerous, too.

Time is both factual and fictitious.

Revenge and vengeance serve a purpose.

We all strive to touch the eternal, to understand the mysterious, to discover who we are.

Pleasure brings peril. Accept it.

You yourself are participating in the evil, or you are not alive.

An eye for an eye makes everyone half blind.

Silence is sometimes loud.

Life is a hot, humid, moody and sensuous tale of
lust, murder, mayhem and betrayal; it traces a
web of secrets and violence.

Do not let reason rule.

We all live in the realm of love and the realm of war.

Fate cruelly creeps across our lives.

Sometimes we fail to recognize the blood, the
sweat, and the dark.

The devil needs no dictionary.

We are all kings and pawns, emperors and fools.

Guilt is a worthless burden.

Life is a cycle, a circle of destruction and creation.

We are all falling deeper into the abyss.

You must destroy and tear down to create
    and rebuild.

Who is to say what is real and what is not?

Danger crouches, around every corner.

As time spins away, the head and heart flood with
    fantastical flashbacks of things remembered,
    real and imagined.

We all walk the road to Damascus.

The fates litter and line the road to our destiny
    with guideposts, obstacles and barricades.

Some people can never be made human.

Harbingers of death are like hulking shadows that
    stalk us in the deep of night, hard to see, and flee.

Our life is but a fleeting moment in the stretch of time.

Regrets cannot be erased.

The tree of evil and the tree of good grow side-by-side
with shared roots.

Love and fear are impossible to hide.

Wisdom sometimes walks with evil.

The world is full of self-hating moralists, visionary
rebels, loose cannons and guilty innocents.

Good fortune is fool's gold.

Into the darkness is where we all go.

Everyone spends a season in Babylon, sometime.

It is an illusion to think you can fool and trick fate;
fate fools and tricks us.

A closed mind is the worst sort of prison.

You must travel outward to come inward, to the
center of your existence.

Violate the rules of realism.

High tragedy and low scandal make the world revolve.

The truth is rarely revealed.

Love itself is a pain, the pain of suffering of being alive.

It is magical to pretend.

The horizon is not so far away.

We all search for truth, for meaning, for significance.

Black is the night.

It is a lie that time heals all wounds. Time deadens us.

Most people are surprised by their own death.

To covet youth makes you older than you are.

Sometimes it is impossible to not feel evil all over.

The hours of hardship are the hours that make
us strong.

Never-ending anger and grief are both useless.

The soul-crushing weight of the world is upon us,
altering us.

Remnants of wasted love, lost love, love that never
was, floating amid a smashed sea of broken
dreams — those are the clever cruel things that
torment and taunt us — turning our souls into
tiny hard shards of stone, living inside a hollow
desperate carcass.

Where the eyes rest, the heart is reborn.

The high life is a dangerous life.

Life is tragic.

Out of the bottom of the abyss comes the voice
of salvation.

The truth can impale you.

Everyone has an impulse for good and an impulse for
    bad, a passion for goodness and an inclination for
    evil; it is what makes people interesting.

Sometimes, we realize, we have already left ourselves.

Many are grifters incarnate, in disguise.

The seeds of Sodom and Gomorrah lie everywhere,
    enticing us, enchanting us, and entertaining us.
    It is hard to look away.

Mirrors mock.

Devotion to darkness and disaster is but a part of
    this broken, fractured, fragmented world.

For a thing to be true, it does not have to be possible.

Life can whittle away hopes, dreams and prayers.

Be a servant to the scarecrows of the inner conviction.

To let our hearts be broken, is to also be healed.

How do we survive immortality of the soul?

If we listen closely, we can hear the sound of that
black and bottomless river flowing through us,
as it ebbs and flows.

Human nature never changes.

You do not have to understand life, for that is
impossible; just experience it.

Nothing is as it appears.

We want things to go on forever, without the pain
of farewells or endings.

There is a roil of harsh light, fog and grayness inside.

Regardless of what is foisted upon us, we can emerge
from the ashes.

We are all touched by the cadences of fairytales.

40 *Days, 40 Nights*

{ 19 }

Faded beauty cannot be denied.

We all search for our holy grail.

To court death and not be afraid, is to live fully.

A deep pain can devour you; it can also push you to great heights.

In the darkest moments, humor can come if you let it.

There are no absolute truths.

Paradise is always perilous.

The mind and heart are such foolishly malleable organs, susceptible and prone to great deceit, trickery and chicanery.

We are mired in the broken layers of humanity.

To be serious and contemplative, is to have a crisis in faith.

You cannot witness the power, magic and mysteries of life without beginning to wonder.

Despair and hope are twin sisters.

In the universe, neither science nor religion has it
   right all of the time.

Sensibility is seeped into the holy fire.

We are born with the sense of our spiritual origins,
   and then we let it be drummed out of us, as we
   drum it out of others.

Everyone loves a portrait of a renegade.

Before we die, clues begin to come back and we
   become pilgrims in a land we once knew.

Life carves up the heart and soul.

The mind is an incandescent thing.

We are learning, we are searching, we are looking for
   reliable witnesses — those who can share their
   story with us in a way we can understand.

The head sees what the heart feels.

All things have breath and are sharing existence
   with us.

In life, there is fate, tragedy and love.

All men know and feel the conflict between forces
   of darkness and forces of light.

The truth is always paradoxical.

Believing in the cycle of life makes it easier to
   respond to another's physical needs.

The heart is an untrustworthy barometer.

Probe deeply into dark pockets, places and pasts.

We are all artists, drifters, dreamers.

Starry nights are so miraculous, you might see magic.

The dark underside is the most exotic.

We are driven to ruin, rage and rapture by bittersweet
   whispers of love and longing.

You cannot always get what you want, regardless of what your mother told you.

We live and approach death in a process of inching toward completion in an imperfect world, knowing that we can never reach it. This is the unending process of seeking life.

The swamp of hell is everywhere.

Smart people surpass the rational and secular — they listen to intuition and feelings.

Life is fragile.

When the mind, body and spirit come together something magical happens.

Danger lurks within.

Life can be raw; still, you must go straight into the heart of it.

Men, gods and devils are but one.

We are born with great empathy, but it can be
  knocked out of us if we are not careful.

There is no safe haven.

How do we identify, or speak of, that longing to
  embrace something larger than this visceral
  present? Something is felt but not grasped?

All things are intangible.

We are pulled toward a collective consciousness; we
  long to be absorbed into something larger than our
  individual human-centered experience.

Look for options, not agendas.

What is sexy is sometimes mutant.

If you bring forth what is in you, what you bring
  forth will save you.

Never let your spirit age.

Out of the flames come many things.

Great webs of sorrow and regret make us bitter
   and old before our time.

The truth does not always sound good.

Many times we are dropped into hell on a string,
   but yanked back like a yo-yo.

Death cuts close and deep.

Tortured souls can cloak and masquerade themselves
   in many coverings.

Many live razor-blade fairytales.

Remember to stop the world and melt into someone,
   or something, you love.

Past pain becomes pleasure.

For whom the gods want to destroy, they first give
   many gifts to.

The search for atonement is long and brutal.

Great glory and fame are often interwoven with
   great suffering.

Blessed people often lead nightmarish lives.

From the time we are born we are looking to
   complete ourselves, spiritually, physically,
   emotionally; we call it "seeking life."

Wrinkles on the soul are not easily removed.

The heart is the seat of much wisdom, thinking
   and emotion.

Lies become truth.

Order and disarray go hand-in-hand in maintaining
   equilibrium, harmony and balance.

To be fully alive, we must cross the threshold into
   terror and ecstasy.

Vanity digs a deep hole, with no end.

Safety is suffocation.

Rarely do we know, realize or understand the full
  weight of another man's burdens.

You have to taste bitter, to know sweet.

Small and great, rich and poor, we all boil and toil
  in the cauldron.

Charm and chutzpah are better than beauty.

One small cloud can eclipse both the sun and moon.

The cobra knows its length.

Nobody can betray you so completely as someone
  you love.

Better foolhardy than a coward.

Darkness and night are the mothers of thought.

There are no gifts. Everything has a price.

Bad people can do good deeds, and good people
  bad deeds.

No matter how long the night, dawn will break.

Deceit in the daylight is harder to see.

He that has embarked with the devil must sail
with him.

Wretched excess is rarely wretched.

Better to die upright than to live on your knees.

Delay increases desire.

What the eyes do not see, the heart does not desire.

The promise of night vanishes in the daylight.

When a heart is weighted against the balance
of truth, it should not be heavy with deceit
and wrongdoing.

Love transcends all, even death.

What we do not understand we fear.

Our misty memories serve to shroud our minds
    and cloak our souls in the dimly burning embers
    of all that has passed.

There are always vultures at your back.

Words burn your tongue the moment they are
    spoken, and they can never be taken back.

Reality does not exist; it is what you make it.

A life lived without passion for something or
    someone is no life at all.

Power spawns madness.

What the naysayers say is not important; the great
    invisible and omnipotent tribe in the sky, called
    "they," whoever and wherever they are, do not
    know everything; they never have and never will.

Grief destroys even a hero.

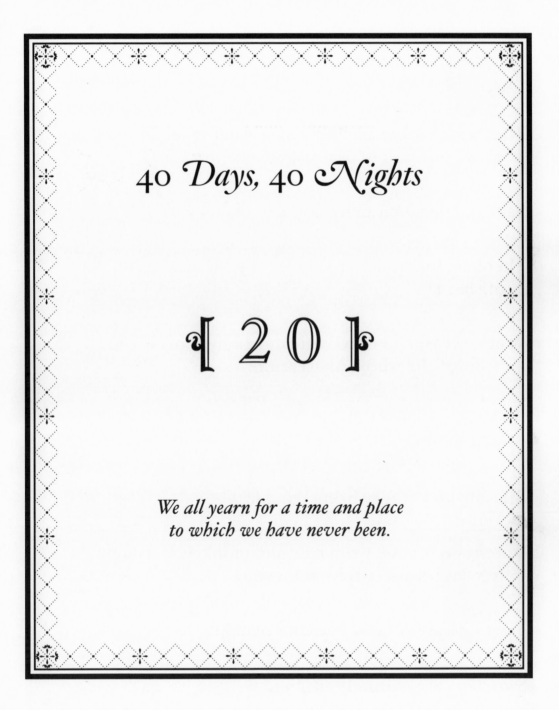

40 Days, 40 Nights

{ 20 }

*We all yearn for a time and place
to which we have never been.*

Lucifer is an enemy who impersonates a friend.

This is a world where nothing is what it seems — a world suffused with intrigue and betrayal.

Pain and pandemonium come in degrees.

There are many vices to stave off guilt and ward off faith.

Whatever you do is evil for somebody. This is the irony of the whole of creation.

Paradise and purgatory are sometimes the same destination.

Bravado and beauty bring trouble.

When you see the palm tree and monkey, the palm tree and monkey have seen you.

There are always tears behind triumph.

Swindlers are naturally suspicious.

Dangerous passages and deep precipices guard
   high places.

Poison pleasures bring pain, eventually, and inevitably.

A good enemy is better than a bad friend.

Where the river is deepest, it makes the least noise.

There is no durable reality, only illusion.

No wise man or prophet, dead or alive, is right all
   the time.

We all walk the halls of hell.

Opinionated persons should be willing, ready and
   able to change their opinions.

Dawn reveals a dark underbelly.

We have all known the malice of heaven.

No one knows whether heaven and hell are faraway
   or around the corner.

Most Edens are invisible.

The beautiful and the damned have much in common.

Resist being terminally trapped in the past.

Scars on the soul and psyche are not readily revealed.

Indiscretion is sometimes the best valor.

There are many saints in the shadows, many shysters
in the sun.

Life and death are inevitable and inescapable.

Every house contains a nightmare swept under the rug.

Who is not drawn to danger?

Some people drink in, and lap up, the bitter, sour
taste of humiliating others.

It is normal to look for love and limelight.

Dreams will tear you apart. Expect it.

Life's troubles are sometimes obscured by
    something far worse.

Pretense is the finest companion of all.

Catastrophes rivet us because they could happen to us.

What defines you also confines you.

The mask of manipulation is faceless and bottomless.

Wisdom is not truth.

Anonymous vipers point the way to unnamed sins
    and seductions.

Everybody runs from something.

In life, be susceptible to seduction.

Growth brings conflict.

Who has not taken a fateful journey into memory,
longing and fear?

Do not obey the script that society writes.

The past does not always let us choose.

Everyone struggles to push back all that is dark
and murky in them.

There are hollow saints and hallowed saints; do not
confuse the two.

It is the spiritually troubled who seek the truth.

The years keep coming, no matter what.

A world of pleasure and pain is made up of peculiar
parallels, passions, poisons and parodies.

Resist time marching on.

In a world devoid of sinners and saints, there could
be no redemption.

The strongest men stand alone the most.

Rosary, revelry and rue make the world go round.

Everybody is at least a little guilty.

Complacency is a thief.

Sometimes the distinction between time and space
    disappears completely.

Close the wounds that scars conceal.

The manacles of truth seldom set you free.

In one way or another, most geniuses are crippled.

There are many private dark holes, sucking us in.

Most people collect tales of misery, loathing
    and defeatism.

Never wash in the sea of self-pity.

We all veer between loving and loathing that which
is closest to our heart.

The dark is never all black.

Lies make you older and colder, until the soul
becomes obliterated and unrecognizable.

Even the stalwart get shaken.

The rare and the beautiful live troubled lives.

Hell's curses are never satisfied.

We all give ourselves away until there are so many
pieces of us that go missing.

The perception of power is power.

We are driven by the dreams and demons that
haunt us.

All is one and one is all.

Everything comes from a void of chaos and emptiness.

The voice in the wilderness is sometimes right.

We all eat of the tree of good and evil, darkness
and light.

The only truth is twisted truth.

As time wanders and passes, only beauty
prevails; the mind forgives, but the heart
holds anguish, forever.

There are many healing poisons.

Beware of lacing fingers with a fiend in human shape.

All things are momentary.

The mind can always be free, no matter what the
body says.

Who has not yearned to shake the pillars of heaven?

The arrogance of fate is fragile.

Poke and prod the dark recesses.

All seek to halt the movement of the sun and moon,
    but none succeed.

The slide into sorrow sometimes gives us wings.

Life is laden with intangibles that make the
    journey worthwhile.

The cure can often kill you.

Defiance defines us.

It is okay to scream and sob, and roll on the floor and
    shake your fist at the sky, and wonder why.

Happiness is perilous and precarious.

Traitors are sometimes heroes defeated.

Many people walk around walled up in their own
    rage and grief.

Taunt and jeer at reality.

Conflicts can kill us or make us strong.

We are stranded in a swamp where chaos and
derangement rein.

Love, grief, pain and loss make us reveal things
about our world and ourselves that otherwise
stay comfortably hidden.

We are riveted by slow-motion highway crashes
and catastrophes.

The more you see the less you know.

Sunset is the devil's twilight.

When the mask of manipulative charm drops,
sometimes we glimpse misery so deep it
feels bottomless.

Once someone survives calamity, the future
looks different; suffering takes on a different
meaning, as does laughter.

The past is never wholly forgotten nor remembered.

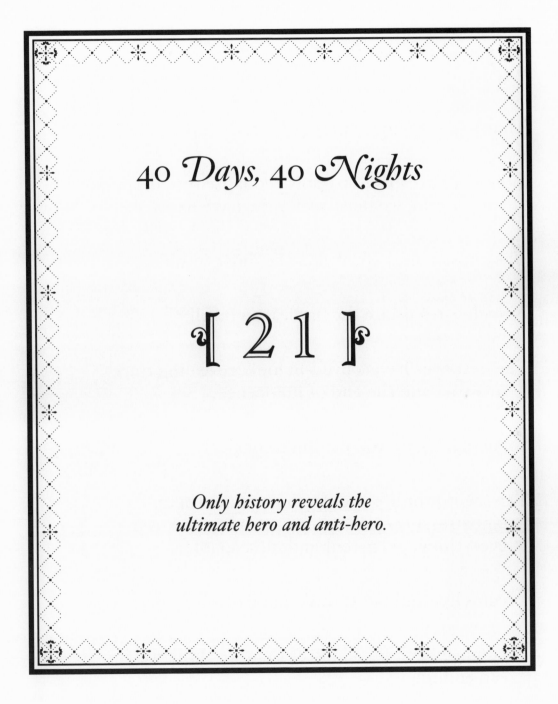

40 Days, 40 Nights

{ 21 }

*Only history reveals the
ultimate hero and anti-hero.*

One who is immune to anguish feels no joy.

Time's winged chariot always catches up to us.

When our dreams of paradise collapse into desperate
rotted ruin, we must seek refuge where we can.

The chosen ones are always the most troubled.

Nameless needs are the hardest to fulfill.

The best eyes have a lived-in look, revealing traces
of a past and the end of innocence.

Some tangles are too painful to inspect.

The sceptor of life and death is always there,
embarrassing us, running up, under, and over
everything, persistent and inescapable.

Dreams live and die at dusk and dawn.

We plunge farther and faster than we think we
can endure.

We are destined to a life of conquest and solitude.

All fortunes fade.

Nobody possesses a spotless mind, heart, or conscience.

We all live with hope and heartbreak.

Those who leave behind the biggest legacy and
    make the biggest mark in life are canonized and
    crucified equally.

Life is a theater of the absurd.

Outrun as long as you can the cruel caress of the
    cold marble tomb that lies in wait.

The heart vacuum is a riddle without reason.

Never wait for the right moment; the moment is
    never right.

Mild-mannered men are capable of great folly.

Pride is perilous.

In life, many worship ruined, crumbling, decaying shrines — and imaginary Edens.

The backbone of love and hate is passion.

All life is a house of cards.

The dreamer's disease is the best affliction to have, as long as there is one dance left in you.

Who actually recognizes the life that they lead, the skin that they inhabit?

The past always refuses to remain buried.

Much of life is but a surreal seesaw, a careening rollercoaster ride to nowhere.

Those with a towering sense of privilege fall hard.

Magic, not realism, is what we crave.

To play with fate is a dangerous game, yet irresistibly enticing.

Deep within, there lies a house of many mansions.

Some echoes never fade.

Our memories contain the pieces of many lives.

The best utopia is that of the mind.

Great adversity always runs parallel to great dreams.

You cannot fix what you cannot face.

The feeble quiver before opinion, the foolish deny
  it, the wise judge it, the skillful direct it.

Most liars eventually believe their own lies.

You use the glass mirror to see your face, the face
  of another to see your soul.

To a valiant heart, nothing is impossible.

We all seek secret places that stir the senses and
  seduce the soul.

Never blindly follow rules.

Sometimes we feel like a stranger even to ourselves.

We are powerless to change the past.

Congratulations and condolences are often the same.

Illusions shatter; memories remain.

The enduring lessons we remember for a lifetime
    are learned in the hardest of ways.

All life is trouble; only death is no trouble.

Only the young, foolish and unwise believe that
    they will never have to compromise.

Black comedy is the funniest.

All lovely lives of masquerade collapse, eventually.

The devil has his martyrs among men.

Bleak and frightening wildernesses hold hidden
    meanings.

The human heart holds many secret recesses.

Life is leavened with humor, freighted with sorrow,
    steeped in history, touched by scandal.

The four walls that house and hold us reflect those
    who reside within.

Never let sleeping tigers lie.

That which is gnarled is authentic.

We must give back, with care, the life which has
    been given to us.

The unspooling of fate holds many knots and
    complications.

All longings and journeys have a consequence.

The saga of truths and deceptions are hopelessly
    entwined.

We are attracted to myth and majesty.

The truth is unkind; so is reality.

Some discoveries go beyond our powers of reason,
but the heart inescapably comprehends what it
cannot understand.

The night is a fickle friend and companion.

You can arise from the shipwrecks and shoals of
the storm.

Most people can survive more than they think.

Pilgrims of the past and present come in many forms.

Sorting through a lifetime of memories helps fill the
void of what passes away.

Do not surrender to life's storms.

What is highly visible is sometimes stubbornly opaque.

Destiny is a fickle friend.

We are beckoned by wounded songbirds that call to
us through the mist.

Sometimes we seek to be alone and wandering in the
depth of our solitude of our misery; however, we
are not alone. No matter where we go, where we
tread, others have been there before.

Anarchy rules supreme.

The promised land is always just a step away.

Each of us has a big black balloon, a darkness
buried somewhere deep inside, swallowing us
up, consuming us.

The enemy and the beast reside within.

If you do not bring forth what is within you, what
you do not bring forth will destroy you.

Deep caves of mystery lie within all of us.

The miracles of this world shine brightly in its sun,
moon and stars.

Ale tipplers and libation lovers laugh loudly, even when they feel like crying.

What you send out, returns to you.

Good taste is one of the worst vices ever invented.

The wise contradict themselves, often.

Alcohol is, from time to time, good therapy for what ails you.

We are all damaged.

The gods and demons forever wage an eternal battle deep within the protective cloak that conceals our ripped and torn, scarred and wounded hearts and souls.

Self-torment is the most painful of all punishments.

It is hard to give up people, places and things that we have forsaken and forsworn.

Fortune is often tainted with sorrow.

We shall never die, not entirely.

Dreamland can harbor many hermetic nightmares.

The wandering stars and heavens above seem so
disheveled and disorderly, but are they?

Eternity gives no answers.

The road to Byzantine is long and perilous.

Dark nights can summon forth dragon-ridden
dreams that make us sweat with terror.

The crystals of time have no beginning, no end.

Wisdom can be cruel knowledge.

Flickering flames and damp desire light humid nights.

Vengeance comes with a price, one sometimes
worth paying.

40 *Days,* 40 *Nights*

❧[22]❧

Some drink and dance to remember,
some drink and dance to forget.

We are all lords of illusion and delusion.

A torn and tattered heart that has been bled dry,
left barren and crumpled can sometimes turn
to stone.

Do not be indifferent to the stars above.

We always love what vanishes, and what has
already vanished.

A small bag of dreams can take us far.

The strong do not run or cower from catastrophe.

A fiery torch-lit spirit can shake the world, change
minds and move mountains; be able to speak up.

We all search for our own truths.

Big people often lead small lives.

Pathos and pageantry frequently come prancing as one.

Our worst fears rarely, if ever, materialize; they are usually, even on arrival, never as bad as we imagined.

What made you bitter can also make you wise.

The conquest of fear yields the courage of life.

When confronted with adversity, we have two choices; succumb or walk through the fire.

Those who forget the past are doomed to repeat it.

Life is a tragic tale of loss and redemption.

Fate is rarely rife with clues.

Polite words without substance mean nothing.

The unvarnished truth is elusive.

Do not stare into the looking glass for too long, or too often, for you might spot the stranger within.

A sacrament of lies always binds people tight.

It is hard to see the inner decay of soul rot.

We report what we have heard in life, when we
    listen to others, since we are merely the
    secretary, the reliable witness.

The worst anger lies seated in the heart.

Fairyland is always very seductive, to all ages.

Invite joy into the heart as often as possible, for
    sorrows lurks in the passage just up ahead.

Pain is for the living.

In the burning embers of firelight, in the flames of
    candlelight, anything is possible.

We are all gravediggers.

Time eventually erodes the glimmer and gloss of all
    things glittery and gold.

Beauty passes quickly, like a phantom dream.

Most memoirs are honey-dipped.

When provoked, who has not been afraid of, yet
    skated precariously upon, the razor-thin broodingly
    attractive edge of slipping into temporary insanity?
    And such fine madness?

Broken dreams can be mended.

The mind's eye is easily fixated on memories that
    never were.

Words and echoes vanish into the wind.

A deep soul makes for haunted dreams, restless
    sleep, and an unquiet mind.

The body senses far more than we know.

A maimed and desolate heart is easily deceived.

Victory and loss are one and the same.

From the sublime to the ridiculous is but a thin
    sliver of distance.

A guilty conscience needs no accuser.

Do not rip down a fence unless you are certain why
it was put up.

Love is a portal to another world.

It is okay in life to rant, rave, reflect and ramble.

A lifetime can be made or broken in a minute.

He who pays the piper calls the tune, writes the
music and commands all to dance.

Burdens of the mind are the heaviest of all.

We leave only shallow footsteps and fingerprints
on the soot of time.

The past is in the present.

Dead men fabricate no truths, gossip no lies.

One man's passion is another man's poison.

Beware, once opened, the secrets of Pandora's box
   are never as enticing.

Life is what is sacred, nothing more nor less.

We never know our fate.

Castles built in the air far surpass those of bricks
   and mortar.

Time rewrites all.

A faint heart never conquers the world.

Handwriting on the wall is easier to ignore than read.

You cannot lose what you never had.

There is evil in the world. Deadly. Relentless.
   Silent. Provocative. Alluring. Irresistible.

Deception and seduction walk hand-in-hand.

Liars are never believed, even when they tell the truth.

What is authentic reeks of soul.

Time alters everything.

All roads lead to the same place. Eventually.

We all question, and lay with, the idea of morality
    and the seductiveness of evil.

In the end the journey is all you have.

Evil is quicksilver, forever shifting shape.

It is difficult to storm, impossible to scale, the
    heights of heaven.

There is no penance of pirates.

A deep, dark cavern lurks inside each of us,
    concealing many secrets.

He who can does; he who cannot, criticizes.

There is an endless river inside, flowing since birth.

We all cry for yesterday.

Do not fear flying in the face of convention.

We all fear, contemplate and grapple with mortality
and what it means to be human.

It is rarely too late, for anything, until you die.

Nothing is written in stone.

The past, present and future intermingle as one
portraiture.

Many things are but a mirrored mirage.

It is always risky to exhume the buried past.

Once we silence and conquer our demons, most
times, they come again.

Symbols teach the meaning of life.

Life's most important lessons and truths are not
written in books.

Nobody owns life's pains alone.

Many of us live with a sense of impending doom.

The world moves in a never-ending circle.

Destiny is never really yours for the choosing.

Mysterious riddles and puzzles abide in many things.

A logical mind is illogically small and narrow.

The truest vision and wisdom lies within, and is
best seen by the inner eye.

Some see the unseen.

To know all is to know nothing.

A coward lies many times over, the aftertaste and
stench of a thousand slow viper bites is always
wafting on his breath, while a bravehearted man
takes the danger of truth on his breath.

Time is a merciless critic.

All seek what is felt but yet not grasped.

There are many dark and cold places of the soul.

Many bright clouds have a darker lining.

Who will rescue the rescuers?

Descent into darkness is inevitable.

Sometimes it is hard to distinguish between the hunter
    and the hunted, the prey and the predator.

The cycles of destiny come and go irreversibly.

Good and evil are both tender and caustic.

It is not uncommon to chase heaven and hell, at
    the same time.

Do not bask in a false sense of security.

40 *Days,* 40 *Nights*

{ 2 3 }

*Fraught times bring a
haunting recognition of
fragility and yet strength.*

Sometimes, the victim is the villain.

Leaping before you look eliminates a lot of worry, fear and procrastination.

To embrace another's heartache softens your own.

Although most sink and suffocate, it is not impossible to swim amid a mire of quicksand.

Your character charts your destiny.

The calendar passes in a blur, but the speed of life is more regrettable to those without passion.

We return to the place from which we came.

The head that wears the crown has riches, but also conflict and heartache.

Only the passage of time reveals and tells the whole truth.

Say what you mean; mean what you say.

The wise can learn from fools, but cannot teach fools.

Destiny does not ignore chance and choice.

Too much remorse poisons life and kills passion.

It is sometimes difficult to see a corroded soul.

Throughout history a pantheon of mythological gods, goddesses, heroes and monsters have fascinated mankind because they illuminate truths and human values.

Fortune fancies the brave and daring.

The path of least resistance is commonly the most disappointing.

A brooding hell and a sparkling heaven can look the same, from a distance.

Sunshine has shadows.

To be human is to be harassed and haunted.

A dark limbo lies deep inside.

Turmoil and loss is a part of everyday life.

Life is filled with, and we are drawn to, timeless
    tales of tragic love.

The sacred and profane often share the same path.

Lies speak louder than the truth.

Our life might be in shambles, but we have just begun.

We all ask, why me?

Sorrow can give wings and wisdom; joy spurs.

Good deeds and blessings come with burdens and
    obligations.

We are all prisoners of our past.

To those to whom the gods give much, much is
    expected.

Drunkenness divulges one's true beliefs.

In life, the deeper you plunge the more curious
    it becomes.

Too much virtue leads to emptiness.

It is hard to face life until you face death.

Who truly understands the secrets of immortality?

The dream should never be abandoned.

Live life to the fullest.

A fool's paradise is better than no paradise.

The brightest and most gifted often meet a tragic end.

We often destroy what we love.

Change usually goes full circle, back to the place
    from which it began.

Troubled waters teach us to swim.

A cynic knows everything, except how to believe in
the unseen, the invisible, and unproved.

We are all reluctant saints and sinners.

Better to meet devils you recognize than those
you do not.

Mirth and merrymaking trump misery.

Dead people hold no grudges.

The Prince of Darkness often comes disguised as a
lady or gentleman.

Most do not taste the poison until it is too late.

False friends are more dangerous than open enemies.

Time devours all things.

Everyone has a dark side, whether it be hidden or
revealed.

Hell is rarely as bad as the road that leads to it.

Silence and darkness are never truly forgotten.

Every genius is a touch mad, a mere step from insanity.

We canonize etchings of what is lost.

The road to hell cuts straight through the heart.

We are always alone, yet never alone.

The world is round, so as not to see too far down the road.

What is tragic is often also triumphant.

One man's wisdom is another man's nonsense.

Man is the most dangerous and illusive predatory creature of all. He possesses many faces, many disguises, such as, pretending to have a heart, soul and conscience.

A joyful eventide can follow a sorrowful morning.

Jesters and prophets wear the same cloak.

In the end, victories turn into defeats, and defeats
turn into victories.

Pleasure and pain come when least expected.

Who is the master of their fate, the captain of
their soul?

Birth is the harbinger of death.

Trash and treasures alike are both appealing,
coveted, and sought after.

Life is a mockery and a lottery.

Excessive behavior marks a full, rich life — rather
than moderation and self-restraint.

We journey alone into a world of loneliness.

It is futile to try and escape from yourself.

All walls can come tumbling down without warning.

Life, love, loss, death and war are never fair.

The poor sometimes feel luckier than the rich, since
    they still believe money will make them happy.

We live amid a fragile and flawed universe.

Sometimes lunacy and madness make sense.

Love of money and lack of money are the root
    of all evil.

One man's misfortune is another's good luck.

Life is a one-way street. There is no choice but to
    keep going forward.

Failure is the foundation of success.

The seemingly simple things in life can be deceptive,
    complicated and complex.

Justice aids and abets injustice.

We argue with the arbitrary, to no avail.

The lord of the manor does not always possess
good manners.

Money cannot buy things that are not for sale.

Social lions are especially cruel, cunning, coy predators.

Can fate and destiny be manipulated?

Foolish men pretend they can stop the clock from
ticking, or that they can at least make it pause;
wise men know this is impossible.

All dreams come to an end.

We are known by the promises we break.

All religions are true and false, right and wrong,
good and bad.

Better to be a sinner than a hypocrite.

Every good has its evil; every pleasure has its pain.

Drink wine for truth and clarity of thought.

Bad and good go together.

Memories make a good companion to loneliness.

Treachery is a formidable foe.

Overindulgence is the best medicine for a hurt heart.

Bring forth the fire within.

Adversity builds strength, stamina, character
and wisdom.

Fear does not make you safe.

Everyone thinks his burdens are the heaviest, and
the worst, weighing the most.

Grief can come through to pair with bittersweet
celebration.

Shards of determination sustain us.

40 Days, 40 Nights

{ 24 }

*Many people are lucky
and unlucky at once.*

*L*ooks are deceptive.

Hell is a desolate wasteland; all the demons and
  devils are here on earth.

The blind do not fear ghosts.

We live for Proustian promises of poetic
  sweet reunions.

Only fools and dead people never change their mind.

Do not be poisoned by fairytales.

Trauma, pain and suffering often pave the path to
  great things.

Failure teaches more than success.

Who among us has not felt, I do not fit in.

In life we lose and leave behind many people,
  places and things, as it is written we must.

Being too civil is totally ineffective.

Trouble and treasure can be found at the end of
the rainbow.

When you die, the suffering is over.

A man's own opinion is more important than
anyone else's.

Love and deceit wear many masks.

Beyond the turbulence and debris, lies a façade
of reality.

A faint heart cannot conquer misfortune.

Both a slandering hypocrite and a slithering serpent
have forked tongues.

Celebrate what you have.

We carve and cut at the world with the knife of
our minds.

Guilt has a million voices that speak many lies.

The best way to learn humility, is to be humiliated.

Innocence is the weakest defense.

We all fly through the inner darkness of our being.

A dash of danger always stirs the soul.

Time is a sly cannibal that devours us all.

Dance when your heart is breaking; dance when
    you feel like crying.

To the valiant, anything is possible.

All geniuses are crippled, in some way.

Nothing is written in stone.

Scoundrels, who live just outside the law, are
    seemingly very appealing characters.

Decay brings new life and rebirth.

Sometimes it is better to run with the devil instead
of trying to run from the devil.

The concept of time is imaginary.

Shock is always in style.

The beauty of the world has two edges, one of laughter,
and one of anguish, cutting the heart asunder.

We unfurl ourselves deep inside.

Many secrets lie in the recess of the deepest self.

"Home" is inside, a place we carry with us.

Sometimes it is hard to tell the difference between
a devil's smile and an angel's smile.

We all cry, bleed, fall down.

Many stare into the dark hole, dim shadows, and
dark phantoms for hours, days, years.

The world is terrible, yet fascinating.

We often dance at the doorstep of depravity.

Great things are born in disaster's wake.

When we fall through the hole inside our own self
there is no end, no bottom.

Many live in the republic of sadness.

Everyone has a different pleasure, passion, pain.

Wrath is a fickle thing.

True meaning can never be expressed with words.

We are all witness to many things.

The fear of pain is worse than the pain itself.

We are not supposed to be perfect.

Cunning little vixens go far.

There is a doorway into yourself, through yourself
and out of yourself.

Many memories refuse to be remembered.

We all teeter and languish, and sometimes bloom,
right on the cliff's edge.

Social butterflies can become vampire bats.

Treacherous pain and pleasure are often entangled,
interlaced as one.

Hatred chokes us from within.

Often we forfeit and ransom the truth buried in
our psyche.

We are all guilty.

The end is rarely an explosion, but more of a
crumbling and falling away, like the edge of a
hole dug in the sand.

You cannot control the uncontrollable.

Which of us has had our desire, our dream, and
then having it, is satisfied?

Demented darkness lives in the imagination.

Sometimes it is good to be belligerent, resilient,
uninhibited, naughty, creative and hilarious.

There is power in humor and madness.

Revivals and comebacks can always precede
the tombstone.

Do not aspire to be a saint.

We are all peculiar, in our own way.

The invisible enemy is the hardest one to believe.

Fate has led the way to this place.

All that we love, all that we are and accomplish in
life, all too soon blows away.

Stardust inevitably turns to cinders.

Even the devil chases his own tail.

Success spawns failure, and failure spawns success.

Empty people are usually full of themselves.

The rich and powerful think the gods are on their
side; many other people do, too.

What you have given, you can no longer lose.

Paint your past any way you like; the more colorful,
the better.

Interesting characters always have conflict.

The playing field is never level.

We all think, we are never as corrupt and wicked as
our neighbor.

The best revenge is being yourself.

Paranoid people are not always crazy, sometimes
they are right.

The heart is hard to rule and govern. But when broken and dipped in sorrow and anguish it gains unflinching fortitude.

Weirdness can be entrancing.

Just because you are paranoid that people are out to get you, does not make you wrong.

When going through hell, keep going.

Famous people are often conspicuously miserable.

Many ghosts live and dance in our heads.

The worst evil springs from the hand within.

Advice is a bitter pill, easier given than swallowed.

Even magicians cannot hide or make the truth disappear, forever; it always resurfaces, eventually, in one incantation or another.

Virtue is its own punishment.

Wise men need fools to follow and listen, and fools need wise men to lead and lecture.

Unseen brooding menace is everywhere.

It is easier to escape ourselves than to know ourselves.

Always dabble in dreams.

It is easy to be a man of your most recent word.

Where there is envy, there is madness.

Transient towns are appealing; one arrives with a tainted past and baggage in tow — yet nobody need know.

Sorrow is a poignant emblem of a life lived.

The untamed passions of drifters and outcasts make for the best lore.

Lunatics make convincing philosophers.

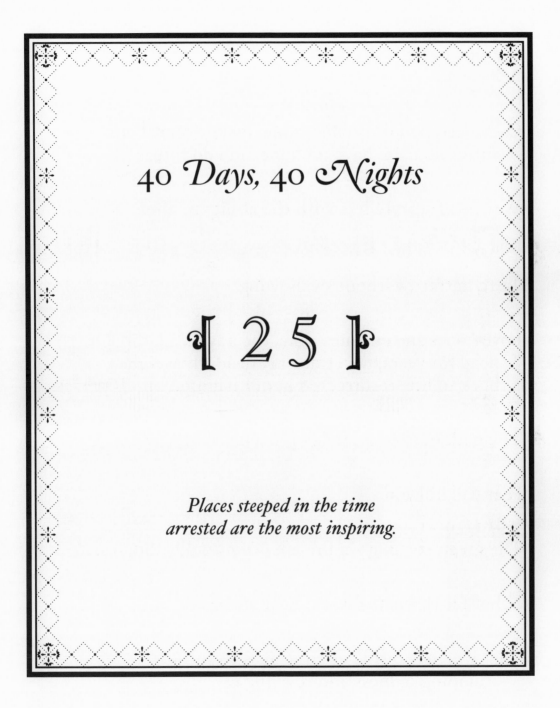

40 *Days*, 40 *Nights*

{ 2 5 }

Places steeped in the time
arrested are the most inspiring.

$\mathcal{E}$njoy joy, it is fleeting.

Only dead people do no wrong, make no mistakes,
   suffer no pain, have no hope, and no future.

We are all storytellers with the ability to alter
   the past.

Taste flattery, without swallowing.

Loved ones and enemies alike, the now dead, though
   dead for years, never do stay dead; they come
   back to life, resurrected in our haunted minds.

The path of excess can lead to a place of wisdom.

Fear will kill you.

The greatest things in life are often totally illogical.

Believe little that you see, hear and read.

That which is inside us continues to surface,
   trumping sadness and reviving us.

With the passage of time, history picks its heroes
   and villains, regardless of who participated in
   the parade or the guillotine.

All lawyers know how to circumvent the law.

What we wish to be true passes for truth.

Those who think they are perfect have the furthest
   to go.

Any idiot can tell the truth, but it takes a smart
   person to know how to lie well.

Life is a dream dance.

It is dangerous to believe your own words.

The truth is so strange, many lie to be believed.

A kite rises the highest when flying against the
   wind, not with it.

Vanity is more dangerous than virtue.

You will not receive praise without envy until you
    are dead.

There is no finish line.

All men breed reptiles of the mind.

Defects and flaws are far more interesting than
    perfection.

It is not difficult to be swallowed up and taken
    down by life's many cesspools, yet, although
    some disappear, not all drown.

Vice makes more martyrs than virtue.

The veil between life and death is thinner than
    you think.

Being first means nothing.

Even though the music plays on and on, few hear it.

Sleep is a thief.

If you lead your life and make decisions trying to
please people, you are not going to do, say, or
accomplish much.

Fear is the mother of many untruths.

A heart knows no boundaries and overshadows all,
even heaven and hell.

Most rise above the sorrow, no matter what.

What is harrowing is sometimes later hilarious.

It is best to know how little we know.

The realm of hell sends warmth and heat to many.

Even sinners can become saints.

What is good in the morning is not always good
at night.

If only for a moment, teardrops make us human
and one with the world.

We all wrestle with darkness.

It is not so difficult to live a lie, but it gets old
and tiring.

Few things are ever as important as you think.

Wealth does not necessarily bring wisdom, serenity
or sentiment.

There is a time for all seasons, even one in purgatory.

It is essential to read between the lies.

Unlike a snake, man does not leave his skin behind.

Silence can be heard.

Time and the wheel of fortune reveal all secrets.

Everyone faces obstacles and disappointments.

Where do the hunted and hunter begin and end?
Who is the hunter and who is the hunted?

In wine there is happiness.

Never let your heart afire grow cold.

Rich people make mistakes; poor people
commit crimes.

True reality is unendurable.

We endlessly consume ourselves with thoughts of
how not to think about things.

A daring rebellious attitude can take you far.

Every face tells a tale.

The rooms in our mind grow smaller and darker.

We find our own grave.

Being smart is not a prerequisite for success, but
an obstacle and hindrance.

The truth can be changed.

Energy is created by belief; when people believe in
    something, it happens.

Life is an Eden of possibility.

A siren's wail has lured many to free-fall plunge
    into the precipice, a place of no return.

Nothing is ever finished but the tomb.

We need thoughts to believe in, to keep us warm
    and safe from the dark.

Passion should run deep.

The sancrosanct and condemned coexist, each
    begetting the other.

We all bargain with the devil, sooner or later.

It is hard to tell the truth without lying.

Secrets and shame can wash away with the rain.

Power is a destructive and cruel thing.

Homes reflect the inner being of the inhabitants.

Despair can run shallow or deep.

As we tend tiny, moral decisions, the soul is not
   sold in one great auction — it is bartered away
   in thousands of tiny trades.

Manifest destiny begins in the human mind.

When we go, it is forever.

Perverse and evil spirits easily penetrate and
   invade all fortresses and minds.

Hardship often proceeds happiness.

There is no simple highroad to happiness or
   misfortune; every man makes his twists
   and turns.

Every heart has its own heartache and secrets.

The greatest hate can come from the greatest love.

Fools and madmen often speak the truth.

What appears tame can suddenly turn wild.

Once across the threshold, the dark forest is never
   as fierce or dangerous as it looks.

Seek to cure what is hidden and buried deep inside.

One lie begets another.

The higher the hedge, the richer the man.

Enchanted is the night.

There is elegance in decadence, and vice versa.

It is impossible to erase or eradicate the desolate,
   lonesome ache inside.

Assume nothing.

The world whirls on its axis, answering to no one,
   swaying to nobody's drumbeat.

Power attracts flatterers, and flatterers feed our
　　delusions, which allows us to hide from ourselves.

It is difficult to unlearn what has been learned.

All knocks can be endured, except the knock of death.

Fear rules the world.

The gatekeepers of fame and fortune are full of
　　fickle and folly.

What is streaked with strife, displacement and vanished
　　innocence forms an exquisitely haunting tableau.

Many walls and prisons of the mind are built with
　　the bricks of religion.

The yellow brick road is stained underneath.

Bitter sarcasm sleeps in silent and sweet words.

We carry secret cargo inside ourselves.

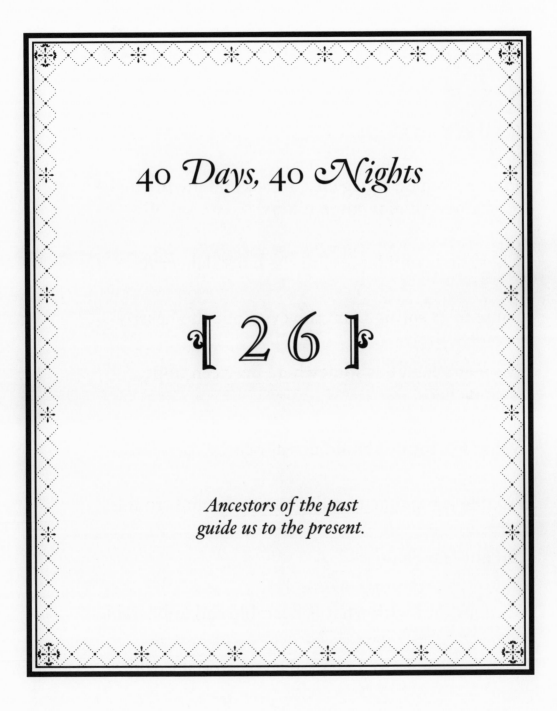

40 Days, 40 Nights

{ 26 }

*Ancestors of the past
guide us to the present.*

*F*ew find or recognize what they are looking for.

Gold keys fit all gates.

Pirates, rogues, renegades, rebels and misfits make
the best dinner companions.

Cherished confidantes are the most dangerous.

Some tears spring from the eyes, not the heart.

No-man's-land lies somewhere between hope
and chaos.

What lies inside should not always be revealed.

No one is immune to pain, heartache and trouble.

Do not fear change.

We must live with what is bearable and unbearable.

It is impossible to disregard the material world.

Lies are sometimes the truth in masquerade.

Devils must be driven out with devils.

Tragedy webs people together with a permanent bond.

Most miracles are small and often unseen.

Spontaneity and surprise are the spice of life.

Many tricks and disguises conceal the void inside.

Beauty is a beast and a burden.

In life, absurdity is not necessarily an obstacle.

Being a fatalist and a fool makes life easier.

What is doomed may be desirous and divine.

Never be overly prudent; to be imprudent is far better.

Fallen angels do not necessarily become devils.

A guilty conscience is better than no conscience.

Defy convention.

Everyone needs a posse of friends.

Do not erase your heart or you will reside inside an empty carcass.

The hand of fate has no soul.

It takes wisdom to laugh at one's own misfortune.

First thoughts are truer than second thoughts.

We are all haunted by something, or someone.

A complete breakdown can lead to a breakthrough.

Everyone rides in a hearse, sooner or later.

The tongue is the most cruel, vicious and dangerous weapon known to mankind.

One deception gives rise to another.

Only time reveals and rules all things.

Anyone who says they have never lied or cheated is
    not to be trusted.

The world belongs to the scoundrel.

Out of nowhere, things just suddenly seem to drop
    into and across our lives like ill-timed curtain calls.

The way to bliss is obscure.

Into the dark forest, into the fire, we go.

We must allow hope to breathe eternal, even if
    nothing else does; as we walk in the light, the
    shadows draw us closer.

Tragedy is intriguing.

A wicked world is short on wise words.

Sometimes it is best to face into the wind.

Take the thief before he takes you.

It is not the years that age one, but sorrow and worry.

The worst hell is a troubled, guilty conscience.

Beauty does not make you happy, but happiness can
make you beautiful.

The looking glass is a formidable enemy.

We are more than we think we are.

All trails lead back to ourselves.

We are all affected by what we have seen and heard,
remembered or not, absorbed unconsciously.

Even heroes can be morally dispossessed.

The devil often lurks behind the cross.

Cynicism is often disguised as wisdom.

The curious are driven to stand on the edge of
the abyss.

We all go down, some deeper than others.

The aggrieved victims of heaven and hell, and
their mutual afflictions, can be seen and heard
in this world.

Home is one's paradise and hell.

The greatest pain and pleasure, paradise and
purgatory, emanates from the head.

What is swallowed by a black hole cannot always
be retrieved.

Even the righteous detour on the road to ruin.

What is going on here? we ask ourselves, seldom
with a reply.

Fortune favors fools, as the anointed darlings and
pets of the gods.

Great importance is placed on unimportant things.

Everyone has it in them to become a monster.

Neither sinners nor saints are immune to pleasures
  of the material world.

We are all captured in our own dragon cage.

Some people's hearts are not in their bodies.

The same man can be both ignorant and wise.

We search for a perfect world, never to be found.

Instinct is the strongest of the senses.

Knowledge can set you free, yet also imprison you.

Roguery and imprudence brings wisdom.

When fortune is good, you rule over the devils;
  when fortune is bad, they rule over you.

Joy is often guarded by the gates of sorrow.

What lies in the subconscious is said in jest.

Some say gilt is good, gilt is godly.

Nobody likes to accept what cannot be changed.

We are always running away from an essential and
    omnipresent emptiness.

Sometimes all roads lead to the same place.

We are never where we need to be, emotionally,
    mentally, or spiritually.

The cycles of eternity are irreversible.

We all resist easily surrendering to loss, or change.

Before you can control the demons outside
    yourself, you must control the demons within.

Good intentions tend to evaporate.

Isolation and lack of comprehension build tall
    walls of intolerance.

The underworld is always close at hand, and nearby.

What is hidden is obvious to many.

Sometimes we need to leave this world behind.

Everything perishes, eventually, only to be reborn.

Good cannot exist without evil and vice versa.

No ointment can heal, soothe, or nurture a
    tortured soul.

Death destroys and heals.

Rich men rarely know the feeling of being
    rich enough.

Never go quietly into the twilight.

Love brings vulnerability and hardness, warmth
    and withdrawal.

Irony is oh so cruel and cunning.

The devil can come as a man of wealth and taste.

Power is the ultimate aphrodisiac.

Comedy and tragedy, laughing and crying spin and
  spiral in an endless circle.

Who can determine what is and what is not to be?

The sun, moon and stars are all imperishable for
  millenia, but we mere mortals are not.

We are our own worst foe and rival.

In life, there is no true safe passage.

We all journey into the underworld, descend
  into darkness.

The end is always near.

All of life's treasures vanish, eventually; some
  slip away slowly over time, others wash away in
  an instant.

If collaboration fails, be confrontational.

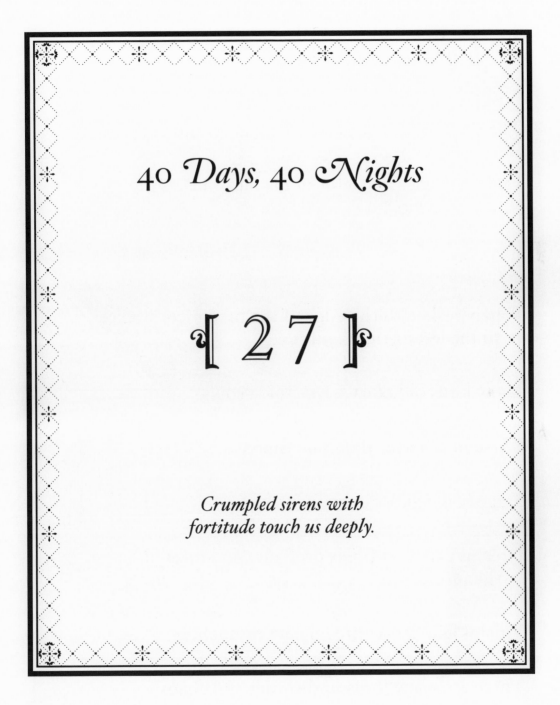

40 Days, 40 Nights

{ 27 }

*Crumpled sirens with
fortitude touch us deeply.*

Victory is never final.

The shadows of the gods can be deep and dark.

Faith, romance and a bit of madness makes life
worth living.

Be fearless.

When pushed to the edge of the precipice, swerve
to the left or right and run.

Many lords of luxury have stolen souls.

Wisdom is better than sanctimony.

Tragedy is a ghost in every home.

Dreams can sometimes prefigure and foretell
the future.

Villains and heroes are equally compelling.

There are many lords of disorder and chaos.

Guilt is a never-ending nightmare, a crusher of
   many dreams.

The devil sometimes speaks sacred writings.

And so, do not listen when "they" say it is impossible,
   it cannot be done, because they have ruined many
   dreams and lives.

The moon sheds its shadow to be born again.

Life dangles, suspended on a mere thread.

Who really knows, or understands, the sequence
   of destiny?

There is power in rainclouds.

Fortune follows him who flees from it, and flees
   from him who seeks it.

There is majesty in the moon.

It is easy to acquire an antagonist, hard to acquire
   a friend.

There exists a mountain of purgatory.

Serpents often guard paradise.

There is mystic bliss beyond pain.

We are all so very thinly tethered to life, space
and time.

Money brings misfortune.

The landscape of the soul is a dark and
dangerous place.

Everyone must come out of exile in his own way.

Doubt is our enemy.

A thread of death and destruction runs through
all life.

Sanity and insanity, success and failure, happiness
and misery are closely linked.

Money moves even the gods.

The heart and eyes are connected as one organ,
    which is the master of the soul.

When luck offers a finger, it is not always wise to
    take the whole hand.

The universe cannot exist without pain, sorrow,
    time, taxes, life and death.

What the eyes see, the heart believes.

The essence of being is forever becoming.

Release from sorrow can be found in many places.

The more one sleeps, the less one lives.

It is hard to tell the difference between heaven
    and hell.

Life is a bittersweet dear grief.

Sweet obessions explode, spewing wickedness.

Rules can be ransacked.

Reverberations and whispers of heaven and hell
    ring in our ears.

Most things cannot and will not be changed.

Lies yield a truth and the truth yields lies.

The netherworld can open up the ground beneath
    our feet.

Faceless serpentine vipers lurk.

We long to be lured for the moment from the
    other side of the looking glass.

Life leads to Elysian fields.

We all dream of special moments sealed in time.

Destruction instigates change.

Who knows whose turn comes next at the wheel?

Most profiles in courage are private.

Sometimes only the head and heart anchor what refuses to give way and vanish.

Love is more than can be seen or caressed.

The forward step of man and time cannot be turned back or even halted.

Relish life.

There is no real escape or victory in life, only a circle with two sides.

We are all a poet of lost loves and things.

There are dark forces in life and human nature.

Certain experiences you never forget, no matter how old you become.

Perfection in life does not exist.

Beware of a reconciled enemy.

Evenhandedness simply does not exist, not really.

Yesterday can eclipse tomorrow.

Many a man reaches reptilian length.

There exists an earthly paradise.

We enjoy seeing through others, but hate being
  seen through.

The ending is never written.

An unsound mind has inspired many a great man.

Understanding is superior to learning.

Even when we do not know what we want, still, we
  are willing to go through hell to get it.

All are born greedy. Most remain greedy.

It is hard to rid the mind of what has been taught.

The mob and the media find us guilty first and
  try us later.

Can fate's decrees be halted?

With desire, comes yearning, fulfillment, heartache.

Too much fear creates distortion and bondage.

Guardian demons and angels sit on alternate shoulders.

There are no absolutes.

Disobedience makes for success.

Turn your back on a wasteland world of "thou shalts."

Money is a hard master.

Crossing over the threshold of a new life is a
    dangerous adventure.

The devil is not always at one's door.

We cannot change the skin on our backs.

The devil knows how to be whispery like an angel.

Words cannot explain what the head, heart and
  soul knows...sees...feels....

Golden seeds do not die.

No night is so long that day will not follow.

The best things lay beyond the reach of words and
  cannot be told.

Nobody can live in paradise forever, for it would be
  taken for granted and cease to be paradise.

Demigods and ideals are dangerous.

Many are consumed by their own pet passions
  and poisons.

Unreal worlds can seem deceptively real.

Death haunts us all, as does bereavement; it makes
  us human.

Every story is different, depending on how you
  look at it.

Few actually catch the dream they chase, as dreams
are an illusive and ever-changing vapor. The closer
we get, they change shape and face, always remaining
just up ahead and barely out of our grasp.

Desire, fear and duty hold us back.

Fragments of memory are emotionally draining
yet mesmerizing.

Those who cannot shake devils off their
backs implode.

We like to glimpse the whispery, slumbering
secrets of others' lives.

Pirate-poets appeal to mutinous hearts,
rebelliousness prevailing over piety.

The end is where we begin as we search for our
holy grail.

We live disguised lives.

40 Days, 40 Nights

{ 28 }

Charmed lives conceal closets of secrets.

$\mathcal{A}$n unlikely journey is the most memorable.

One cannot prepare for danger; it prowls in
    unexpected places.

We all search for the river of dreams that flows
    through the promised land.

You cannot make someone love you.

The past that was, as well as the past that never
    was and never will be, haunts us.

Being reckless is good.

The heart understands more than we think.

Sometimes the shadow is a sanctuary, a safe haven,
    a place to escape the cruel taunting light with
    its accusing, mocking eyes.

One man is not bad because another is good.

A heavy purse can be a prevailing curse.

There is but a thread between a mystical experience
and a psychological crackup.

Imperfection makes us not supernatural and
immortal — and that is lovable.

Betrayal is the worst hurt of all.

In life it is always good to fashion fire in the head.

Heroes are flawed, as are villains.

Many knew your face before you were born.

Life — all life — is sorrowful, no matter.

Draw your own line in the sand.

Broken promises turn us to stone.

Storytellers often tell the truth.

The clearest vision comes from seeing with your
inward middle eye.

All are not friends who smile at you.

Sometimes we hurt ourselves to see if we still feel.

Destiny cannot be foreseen.

Many things are engraved upon our hearts and souls.

Nobody ever can be the person they were.

There is chaos and anarchy in the world, forever
    and always.

We cannot escape what has passed before us.

Greed is a poor imposter, but a great imitator, of
    true passion.

Time can slice and sever the soul.

We all have inner problems, inner mysteries, inner
    thresholds of passage.

Every reflection tells of memories.

To endlessly fear, worry and obsess about old age
and death makes time go all the faster.

Life bites deep.

We all need to tell our story, and to understand
our story.

There is no wrongdoing in an empty house.

One who tells you about others will tell others
about you.

There is no safe shelter from the storm.

Deprivation and suffering open the mind to what
is hidden to others.

There is a beast, a dark savage inside.

A hero has a thousand faces.

Death is best viewed through the eye of desire
and fear.

He who lives with a devil, becomes one.

There is a universal need to connect with tragedy
and mystery.

One knows not the stability of his life.

We all take backward voyages, through the
turbulent tides of our inner sea.

Nothing is everything.

To scale the heights of heaven, or to plumb the
depths of hell is a perilous journey, indeed.

Wealth brings worries.

The world remains infatuated with bad boys who live
hard, fast and free — those who refuse to conform
to the codes and conventions of society.

We are all morally and mortally ailing.

Tomorrow is promised to no one.

Breaking the ideals and idols of society is the path of the mystic.

Life unfolds itself in its own time, whether we want it to or not.

The worst hell is to be dropped into the snakebite deep within.

Who can compete with the realm of the gods?

The doors of perception are wide yet narrow.

When the walls of the world open up, jump the chasm; it is not as far as you think.

The end of our good begins our evil.

Some things which are discovered, are beyond our power to understand or explain.

Great power is inherent in us all.

The origin of great success is often deeply rooted in a painful past.

Society puts its mask on us.

The gods have a weird and warped sense of humor.

Better an open enemy than a false friend.

We come out of, and go back into, the darkness.

Flattery should never be mistaken for praise.

The hours of trial make us strong.

Happiness resides in the silhouette of sorrow.

The ghosts that inhabit our heads live in a place
    beyond time, and space.

Light always has the shadow of nightshade.

No paradise is without sweet suffering.

We hate in others what we hate in ourselves.

The murky waters of morass surround the world.

One devil knows and befriends another.

The heart has reasons that reason knows not of.

A glance at death kills all innocence.

Tend to your own demons before you crusade
    against your neighbors' devils.

Wise people can also be wild and cruel.

Unseen realms and other lifetimes are always nearby.

There are many shades of illusion and false impressions.

We find the passage to take us through times
    of challenge.

Most heroes are silent.

There are moral hazards hidden everywhere.

Everyone swims in the sea of broken dreams.

Humor saves us.

There is always yesterday, but not always tomorrow.

Rely on intuition, our true being.

We must let go of all we seem determined to
hold on to.

Everyone has a thousand stories.

Another person's life is never as pretty as it looks
from the outside.

Shadows stalk the night.

Fate will find you, regardless of where you hide.

In thinking, the majority is always wrong.

Love thine enemies because they are the instruments
of your destiny.

Fear, lust and duties dominate the world.

The field of time is short but endless and indefinite.

What you run from will chase you.

Most things human beings like best are either
immoral, illegal, dangerous or deadly.

Indiscretion is the best type of discretion.

Make trouble.

To understand that we live with the presence of
death, sharpens the appreciation of life.

Charm can neither be bought, nor borrowed.

Nobody is a beauty queen forever.

Some people wish with all of their heart that they
could take you all the way down with them.

Every picture hides a story.

We poison ourselves, slowly.

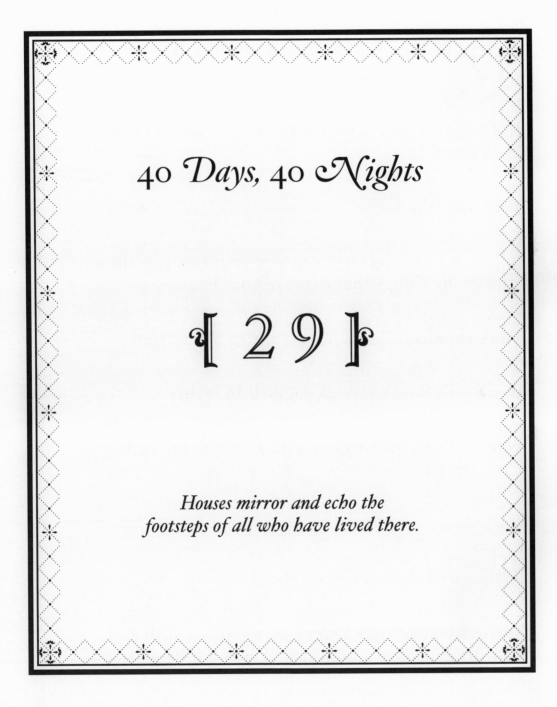

40 Days, 40 Nights

{ 29 }

*Houses mirror and echo the
footsteps of all who have lived there.*

*D*o not be afraid to reinvent yourself.

Are ruthless people happier? There is only one way
to know.

Take back the night.

In life, many things will capture your eye; pursue
only the things that capture your heart.

The best way to learn honesty, is to be cheated.

It is hardly wise to steep yourself in reality.

When the eyes see too much evil, there are calluses
on the heart.

There is a secret world inside all of us.

Prosperity is a treacherous thing.

Those who have not known torment, anguish and
heartache have a diminished view of the world.

The truth is often manipulated.

It is easy to become enslaved in a chain of pain.

To be jealous of youth makes you old.

He that has no enemies has no friends.

The highway to hell and the highway to heaven
   often lead in the same direction.

Death is a patient predator.

Inspire change.

Lunatics can become legends.

Those able to outrun silent shade and shadows of
   fate learn strange secrets.

Happy hour begins on the highway to hell.

A life well lived is shambolic.

Deviate from the path expected.

Many trials are delivered to our front door each day.

A liar is always in recovery.

Life is but a reflecting mirror, a memoir of madness.

We live with death trailing us.

A man without convictions, regardless of what
    those convictions are, is not a man at all.

The murky terrain of the mind is an abyss.

Palaces bring peril.

We always do come fatally full circle.

A slow drop into despair is the hardest way to drown.

To envy riches makes you bitter and miserable.

Embrace fear.

Great souls take on the task of change.

There are many unholy ghosts and noontime demons.

It is not unusual to live a ragged life filled with
    disappointment and betrayal.

We are our own prisoners.

Fire in the head makes for a life of ashes and
    half-burnt embers.

What motivates us can destroy us.

It sometimes tastes sweet to drink a bitter cup of fury.

Triumphs are often accompanied by tragedies.

Moods of the mind are quite maddening to all who
    partake and observe.

Evil is powerful, but so is love.

Some life choices, once made, cannot be undone.

The demons within are our own downfall.

Sometimes cruelty is easier to understand
 than kindness.

Promises made in the dark are rarely kept.

Innocent men bear the scars and sins of the guilty.

Confront chaos.

If you never change your mind, why have one?

Sober sorrow is the most painful.

The excess and extremes of human behavior make
 life interesting.

Diabolical forces come to us in many forms.

Pain tells, and reminds us that we are really alive.

There is menace in mystery.

Life is but a temporal mirage reflected in the
 waters of time.

Time strips us down and makes us naked.

Enjoying life is far more important than stacking
up wealth and fame.

Wicked can be wonderful.

Life is a master magician, a master at disguise.

We are all gods and generals of our own destiny.

How do you unmask the truth?

Excess leaves an empty space inside.

If you cannot scale the wall, blast through the wall.

The invisible lies behind the visible world.

We can all transform ourselves into something
greater than we are.

Dance in the streets.

Flak and disapproval strengthen resolve.

Until there is no breath, it is never too late to be
what you never were.

Sometimes bad behavior is good.

Man does not like reading the handwriting on
the wall.

The world is flat and round, at once.

We see what we project upon people, places and
things, not what is really there.

Having a goal and purpose is never seedy.

Our eyes add a thin coat of varnish and gloss to
most things.

Time erases and destroys all things.

Ignite the senses.

We are all actors, with the whole world as our stage
to play and make-believe in.

Ride the carousel as far as it will take you.

The rich suspect the poor, and the poor suspect
the rich.

If you cannot convince people, confuse them.

Chains of gold feel no better than those of brass.

Slothful is the slave of covetousness.

Do not eat from the bread of shame.

Sometimes it is as hard to remember as it is to forget.

Virtue is rarely as respected as money.

You can never find the passageway back to the
place where you were before.

There is a season for revenge.

High heels are the best form of transportation.

Chaos erupts in a split second.

Smooth seas do not make skillful sailors.

True devils and demons rarely appear as the Prince of
Darkness except in the movies and at Halloween.

It is easier to exist than to live.

Many things are born out of bitterness, jealousy,
revenge and rage.

Consult your soul often.

The best decisions are made between you and
yourself, not between you and them.

Naysayers usually have nothing to say.

Life is too hard if you see it clearly.

Anger, judgment and secrets rule many moments.

The wheel of fortune can be reinvented and
manipulated.

Epiphanies come in small measures, often unrealized.

The depth of cunning knows no limits, nor boundaries.

Meaningless priorities fill many minds.

You have to live with yourself. For a very long time.

Greed grows greed.

The heart is an ironic thing.

Magic rises out of the horizon, especially at dusk.

To surrender is always difficult.

Loneliness and longing are not always recognizable.

If you believe in the land of milk and honey, you
    will find it.

Grace and grit lead the way to tender mercies.

Convenient lies cement the world.

40 *Days*, 40 *Nights*

❧[30]❧

*Old stories and echoes are
remembered and relived.*

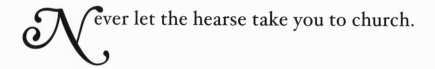Never let the hearse take you to church.

Beware of things that bite without a care.

If it does not affect you in the heart there is no connection, no consequence.

Everyone has a story to tell, to those who will listen.

Sometimes the whole world is wrong.

Do not worry who hears you sing or what they think.

Troublemakers have fun.

When death knocks one does not wish for more money, only more time.

Privilege brings dysfunction.

Few find the life for which they have waited their whole life.

There is dark of day and black of night.

Use the power of your voice.

Life plunders mythology for its tragic-comic landscape.

The past is never finished.

Interesting people have faults unresolved,
    personality unstripped.

Poor people with rich friends end up poorer.

The things you avoid will catch up to you.

Peering through the two-way mirror of time
    all is rewritten, commingled as we see, dream,
    and imagine it.

Our truest self lives in shadowland.

Great power often springs from a painful past.

Those who dance are not afraid of looking like
    the fool.

Dreamweavers excite the world.

Pain and passion are best not kept bottled up.

The past speaks louder than the future.

What is thought forever lost can be rediscovered.

The devil's darlings are given wings.

Arrogance breeds stupidity.

Heroes have many enemies.

The plundering and pilfering of the ages takes its
toll on us.

Saintly behavior can conceal the devil within.

The undercurrents of sadness can come crusted
with a fine tipping of jollity.

Victory surmounts loss.

The roots of deception run shockingly deep.

A track record is meaningless.

We are our own worst and best false prophet.

Memories take many forms; they do not match
    real life.

All dragons and swine seek pearls.

We also loathe what we love.

Happiness is highly overrated. Misery is highly
    underrated. You cannot have one without the other.

What sets you free, can also imprison you.

A big black hole, always nearby, beckons us.

It is with wary regret that we grapple with life,
    death and the heart's travails.

Even heroes hunger for something more.

A myriad of minstrels and misfits give life color
    and heroes.

Life is full of strange gods.

An emotional wilderness is a landscape pockmarked
with craters, full of shadowy recesses.

Time is a fragile flawed fortress.

Find comfort in the shadows and darkness.

Those who put walls up have to live inside those walls.

Defiance is a form of obedience.

Life is a terminal condition. Nobody survives forever.

The best man does not always win.

What seems to come from nowhere sometimes
comes from out there.

All are born with an envious nature.

Emptiness reigns in many souls.

Food and drink help to ease the pain of whatever
nightmares assault you.

Even walls of gold and silver tumble down.

Anonymous anonymity is good for doing good, as
    well as bad.

Happiness overshadows heartbreak.

People feel passionately about what they love
    and hate.

Life can be rewritten.

The cult of common sense does not always
    make sense.

Love and hate make passion.

We journey alone into a world unknown.

No one hears the echoes of drops from fallen,
    wasted tears.

There is viciousness in fate.

What a man makes is there for another's greed.

Never dance upon the grave of the departed.

There are moments in life when we encourage
madness and welcome insanity.

Some wounds will not go away.

We live beneath a wicked sky of a lonely night.

Do not be afraid to walk in the shadows while
everyone else walks in the light.

Life is a funeral lullaby.

Who has not been deserted by departed
despotic gods?

Beauty is a depreciating asset.

The past absconds with our hearts and souls.

Pain is never a world away, but more likely close
at hand.

Court counterculture ethos.

You never know what you might find behind
the façade.

We all want to know, who do we blame?

Envy and jealousy often arrive cloaked in smiles
and praise.

A cycle of fear is contagious.

Many sit unhappily in their mausoleums.

Fear follows us, doom hovers just around the
corner, like a dark cloud.

Defy orthodoxy.

Many people reside in palaces of vanity, theaters of
self-love.

Priests bless themselves first.

Unfulfilled yearnings are with us, always, seared
into our souls.

He who has the funds will find the friends.

The duality of the beauty and the beast always go
    together, as one.

Sweet and sinister coexist.

There is always truth in fiction, and fiction in truth.

We are afloat on a tiny ship filled with fools.

Life makes us dispossessed and haunted.

We fool people into believing we are sane.

Your shadow is the only one who walks beside you.

Some say, the higher the house, the worse the
    storm, but this is rarely true.

It is hard to cut ties with all of the lies in which we
    are living.

A snake is not killed by its own poison.

Time changes everything.

Downtrodden beauty is often opulent in its
melancholy, loss and optimism.

A wound heals but the pain lingers.

The moon is a fine thief of errant hearts.

Within the hidden catacombs of our own hearts is
where the real danger lies.

The root of all happiness lies in the mind.

Friends can be enemies and enemies can be
friends.

The eye only sees as much as the mind allows.

It takes courage to open our eyes to the world, to
see what we would prefer to ignore.

There is not always a white light in blackness.

40 Days, 40 Nights

{ 31 }

When you hear the
music, do not resist.

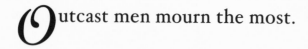

Outcast men mourn the most.

Nothing stops tradition.

Valor, faith and hope govern the world, not kings or heads of state.

Those who think they are invincible make a tragic mistake.

Golden-haired treachery runs rampant.

Once something grabs hold of the heart, the fingerprints are always there.

Scarlet people leave a mark on history.

It is impossible to purge the past. It seeps back.

Survivors are often uncompromising.

Heartbreak alters everything.

What makes life worth living, we wonder.

Calamity leaves a hefty fingertip on shaping
    the future.

An irreverent approach often works.

You can never be sure of what you see and what
    you think you see.

At times everyone dips his or her toes into the
    devil's water.

We all chase our shadows.

Nothing is de facto.

Those that bathe in envy devour themselves and
    destroy the world.

Madmen and mystics mourn the deepest memories.

The truth is fallible.

Solace is a state of mind.

No pair of eyes ever sees the same picture twice.

To ponder life can be quite terrifying.

Good fortune is precarious and transient.

To be alive is to know the string of cold, dark
    orbits and collapsing stars.

Decadence is compelling.

Beyond the fossils, the folds of a past littered with
    loss, we reinvent the future.

There is a confluence of tragedy and triumph.

We are all obsessed by, and run from, death
    and desire.

Everybody's heaven is different.

People with deep thoughts, feelings and consciences
    experience thunder and lighting in the head, and
    knives in the heart.

The promised land is everywhere.

It is not unusual to sometimes think there is
    someone else inside my head, that is not me.

Some things are beyond words and pictures.

The world's smart set, of people, are often
    insufferable bores.

It is wise to be wild and unfettered.

The presumed and supposed best and brightest are
    rarely the best and brightest.

A dark night conceals evil and enemies.

Stately pleasure domes are alluring, and inviting,
    but deceptive.

The vapors of chaos permeates all.

Once somebody touches us, and our life, the
    footprints are always there.

We crave and carve what we do not have.

Avoid people who fall prey to a proliferation
   of pretension.

Bad things can lead to good fortune.

An insular world is suffocatingly small and narrow,
   with far too many boundaries.

The perverse and drop-dead decadence fascinates us.

Everything has a false bottom.

The stars in sparkleland shine bright, so it seems.

Many people are born emerald green and malcontent.

Why are we drawn to villains and villainesses?

The world is filled with sadistic nuns and
   sardonic puppets.

It is good to be gaudy and gauche.

Anything is possible in the ruined palace of
   the mind.

Wise men pick their weapons carefully.

The walls of hell are always closing in.

Court chaos.

The worst pain in life is rarely as bad as the fear
and dread of it.

We all go into the inferno, eventually.

Things always change, until we stop changing, and
then we will stop living.

People who do not love animals have no soul.

Extreme caution brings neither safety nor security.

Our greatest hope is our greatest fear.

If all of your wishes were granted your dreams
would be demolished.

What you save can also destroy you.

Defiance of death defines us.

Recipients of largesse often cease to be grateful.

White light luminosity always has a dark shadow side.

Parables and prophecies often speak the truth.

Darkness conceals and liberates us.

Life is alternatively tragic and comic.

Pretty paradises consume more souls than
    supposed Satans.

What is seductive is also destructive.

In the landscape of the world, everyone and
    everything is small.

Question authority.

Life's detours are good.

Escape and bypass the boundaries.

396

We are all trapped in velvet venomous boxes of our
own making and design.

A wound may heal, but there is always a scar.

Who is the predator and who is the prey?

To live fully, one must tempt death, and fight
demons real and imagined.

We are shaped by the night.

Power wants more power.

We are made up of the fine fragments and
splintered shards of our life.

The littlest things are the hardest to let go of.

What the heart knows, and the eyes cannot
conceal, the head hides and denies.

Do not always play by the rules.

Many people are naturally attracted to the underdog.

We are bound by the life we left behind.

Life itself is a pilgrimage; every day can have a
    magic moment.

Deep in your soul you know your dream.

In the end we are alone, always.

All life is filled and fraught with secrets, lies and
    betrayal lurking just below the looking glass.

Never strew roses or pearls before swine.

Time illuminates triumphs and failures.

Consensus is evil.

The past haunts and imprisons us all.

Few who enter through the door of miracles
    recognize where they are.

Envy fires up hate.

What would life be without secrets, lies and betrayals?

Life redeemed is an encircling spiral.

The night has its own ethos and language.

In life, there are always moments of merrymaking
and joy wrapped in the backwash of miseries.

We are all the clown, the ghost, the queer one,
the outsider.

No one knows for whom the dark clouds gather,
and the clangor of a funeral bell rings out, until
it is too late.

When the bitter wears off, you get used to it.
Sometimes.

Contempt can smolder, insidious beneath the surface.

The spirit of a renegade is engaging.

40 *Days*, 40 *Nights*

{ 3 2 }

*Our childhood colors the
portrait we paint of our lives.*

*D*reams foretell lies.

There is a dark side to enlightenment.

If you do not follow your heart you become bitter.

Compromises and cruelties drive the world.

A ladleful of emotions, remembrances and
    dreamscapes with no expiration date helps
    renew and regenerate us.

The present is culled from the past.

No one can stand in the middle of a deluge and not
    be carried to a new place.

Everyone has a touch of larceny and original sin.

Life is laced with lust, envy and tragedy.

Benevolent demons and devils seem very attractive.

Fight the fears that hold us close.

A soul travels a dark and dangerous road, a perilous
    path, on its journey from dust to dust.

Evil must be driven out by evil.

Sometimes we need to evaporate and disappear
    from ourselves as well as from this world in
    which we live.

All towers crumble in a tragic way.

The mouth of greed and covetousness is never full,
    until it is filled with dirt from the grave.

In the darkest hour, comes the light.

When it comes to people, places and things
    we have loved and lost, sadly we play that
    same tape in our head over and over again,
    of forever haunting flashes, visions, sights,
    sounds, smells and memories....

All of life is déjá vu.

We burrow into the marrow of darkness.

When death comes the rich have no money, the
poor have no debts.

Time betrays all.

Staring into the void, time is frozen.

There is joyful sorrow and sorrowful joy in the
knowledge of life.

Everything is temporary.

To survive calamity, death and destruction, is to be
reborn stronger.

Imperfections are interesting and intoxicating.

Time erases, consumes, destroys and devours many
things, including itself.

Palaces are prisons.

The fates escort the one who will; the one who will
not, they toy with then tow underwater.

Perfection is not lovable, endearing, or enchanting.

In order to move forward, we mine the misery and
the magic.

To be sensitive is to be full of pathos.

Into the lion's mouth we all go.

Time is not always a traitor, nor an enemy.

Man sees others as devils, not his own reflection in
the looking glass.

Tear rules of realism into confetti.

Smudges on the soul are easily concealed but
not forgotten.

What is bizarre is yet strangely familiar.

Sometimes we have wings inside, broken wings
that no longer fly.

Harness the dragon inside.

Beware when the fates send gifts; they lullaby you
to a deep-seated sleep until you awake alone and
shivering, with all ripped away, clutching the
ashes of yesterday.

An army of one can change the world.

Everyone should be carried away on the wings of
madness, at least once.

Combustible people create excitement.

Time accelerates as it goes.

A soul that is deep has been singed and scarred by
the burning cinders of a dying fire; the embers of
pain, fear, anger, regret, love, loss and uncertainty.

Troublemakers stir and move the world.

Personal gods and mementos are poisonous and
not great to all.

Desire is crucial to a well-lived life.

The smoldering fire inside seeps deep, searing the
    marrow of our bones.

No one is alone with their losses.

Tragedy and chaos does not always give way to
    humanity and compassion.

Looks should not rule your life.

We are the cause and creator of most of our own
    personal paradises and prisons.

The gods favor the bold-faced.

Gorgeous ghosts haunt our heads.

The world rotates, spilling hate and love,
    judgment and mercy.

Life is a journey of chaos.

A portrayal of the time, a portrait of the past, is a
    betrayal of truth and fiction.

There are many levels of truth.

You do not have to be a seer to see a sign or to
sense a prophecy unfolding.

There is truth in the wisdom of fools.

Who will be the savior of the broken, beaten,
beautiful and damned?

There is no real cure for pain and passion.

It is rare to see the real person behind the
outcast mask.

Time erodes all.

Most are willing to risk the wrath of the gods to
get what they want.

The battle between good and evil is never won.

When we try to pick off and peer beneath the
layers, more scabs fester and scars develop.

In the ruins is where the home of our heart lives.

We are all imposters and tricksters.

All heroes are haunted.

From the wreckage is where we recover long-missing
   parts of ourselves.

The past is never far away.

Anarchy and chaos bring moments of compassion
   and anguish, mercy and madness.

The rain falls on the just and unjust.

A snake in the grass is hard to spot.

Demons of the night that call and beckon to us are
   usually enticing, sensuous and seductive.

A friend to all is a friend to none.

The rank smell of decay and mildew closes in
   on us, eventually.

Life is imperfect.

Angels smite and slay us as mirthlessly as devils do.

Fortune is fickle.

Our lives are tangled in ways we do not foresee.

To he who is born, death is certain.

We all have a dark, dangerous instinct, a primitive
instinct to survive.

Perfection is inhuman.

Love, lust, greed and hate can make sane people
temporarily insane; sometimes permanently.

All paradises are false and temporal.

When passions spill over and the mind runs
rampant, anything can happen.

Buying is not the same as acquiring.

The mind is a fragile thing to trample, but so is
　　the heart.

We conjure up our own reality.

Both love and death stalk us in the strangest of
　　places, ready to spring when we least expect it.

Nothing ever looks as good up close.

The greatest destruction and evil comes from within.

Splendor and cruelty come hand-in-hand.

Love and death lurk and nobody is immune to the
　　biting sting of either.

When the world comes crumbling down, we are
　　swept up in the fight of our lives, even if it is
　　only in our head.

Sometimes it is necessary to jump into the abyss.

40 *Days*, 40 *Nights*

❧{ 33 }❧

Overindulge today,
delay tomorrow.

Sultry days and clandestine nights captivate us.

Moments of truth and enlightenment do not come
quietly; we are hurled into them.

All goodbyes are false and fleeting.

Scars on the soul and the body are restless souvenirs
of the past.

Our roots define us.

Betrayal strips us down with the sensation of cold
black wings folding around the soul.

The human heart is a furtive and murky place.

When falling through time and space, it is best to
embrace the blackness.

The collision of fate and destiny is a patient process.

Devils dance on water.

No one gets into trouble without his or her own help.

Eyes are the scouts of the heart.

Dreamland can be a grotesque and nightmarish place.

Be disobedient.

To be kissed by genius is to be kissed by insanity.

We are all heroes and saviors.

Psychological terror and erotic possession are
closely linked.

Nobody escapes falling back into the past.

The only thing worse than not getting what you
want is getting it.

Do not grieve over the unavoidable.

Man is a beast of prey.

We cannot stand guard against pain forever.

The finger of fate can move slowly or quickly
across a life.

Who knows the truth? No one does.

The world is inhabited by nameless silver-tongued
serpents.

We erect the walls of our prisons.

Most splashes of horror are kept tucked from sight.

The truth hides in unlikely places.

Love belongs to those who choose to love in the
face of the keen awareness that none of us ever
really know or understand another person, ever.

There are no real horizons, only a mirage.

What the devil brings, he also takes away.

He must stand high who would see the end of his
own mangled destiny.

Let the demons sleep undisturbed, because once a
person digs deep, awakening and uncovering the
covertness that lurks beneath, you could discover
that untold darkness lurks deep, embedded within
your very own heart.

Follow your passion.

No chaos is casual in real life.

When you struggle in quicksand, you sink faster.

The face is the mirror of the heart and soul.

We must slay the dragon inside.

You either live in a world you think is based on
manipulation, or you can live in a world of trust;
you cannot live in both.

Voices in the head often tell the truth.

Foreboding places plunge the heart and soul into the
darkest depths of unfathomable pain and pleasure.

In this life, there are many choices of evil.

Prayers rise and fall, often best left unanswered.

To fail to prepare is to prepare to fail.

Disturbed damsels in distress attract many suitors.

Once we uncork and unleash the powers that lie
hidden within, they cannot be recalled.

Sometimes you have to be blind to see clearly.

The footprints of age can make us ageless.

Although the whirlwinds of calamity and catastrophe
sweep over us like out-of-control wildfires, the fury
of our flames can allow us to arise from our ashes,
for another cycle of life and living.

Never let your voice be silenced.

You are a master, mistress and servant.

Unlikely people change history.

Fairytales are delicately dissembled and varnished
nightmares.

A soul that swims in the midnight of dark sadness
is a tinderbox ready to ignite.

The dark night of the soul comes before the light.

Adversity builds strength.

The lion of self discovery kills the dragon monster
of thou shalts.

No matter how low you fall, you can fall lower.

There is a light that shines on all things dark.

We are but haunted ghosts stumbling and staring
deep into our past, a place filled with apparitions
of the faces we have been, the masks we have
worn, the places we have lived, the people we have
loved and lost.

Good and evil are always in conflict and unison.

When one door opens, another closes.

There is a place beyond pain and pleasure, gain and
loss, fear and desire, you and me.

Yesterday can never be left behind.

The sun continues to shine behind the clouds.

It is possible to wander the darkness without
getting lost.

The heart is the seat of intellect and the source of
thought, which the tongue speaks and serves to
make real.

It is therapeutic to put realism on hold.

A sense of security is a false thing, a twisted
illusion; there is no security in life, period.

The devil always wears a new disguise.

We have to talk to our hurts, as if they were
real people.

To thine own self be true is good advice rarely followed.

All tragedies seem senseless.

We must go beyond pleasure and pain, love and
hate, wisdom and ignorance, health and
sickness, good and bad.

Blackness seeps into the chest, unseen.

The eyes of intolerance are blind.

No matter what, we all get swept along into the
center of the vortex, tumbling deep into the
abyss, despite our own hardheaded and rather
inflexible will and intentions, kicking and
screaming the whole way.

There is no beginning, middle, or end.

Great power comes from following a painful path.

Loss and change, pain and suffering, do indeed lead
to growth and enlightenment.

Explode convention.

The only way to describe a human being truly is by
    describing his imperfections.

A lie unchallenged becomes the truth.

The secret cause of all suffering is mortality itself,
    which is the prime condition of life. It cannot
    be denied if life is to be affirmed.

Grief is an illusive omnipotent thing.

The higher we fly, the farther we may fall.

Some things that are obvious to our senses
    remain invisible to and beyond the reach of
    our rational mind.

The truth always comes with a twist.

It is sometimes good to nurse a grudge.

The heart, soul and spirit were invented to humiliate
    the brain and body.

Everyone goes away in the end.

We are the vortex of our own hurricane.

Until death anything can happen, anything is possible.

Cruel destiny always tracks us down and finds us.

The price of being alive is that one day the stars
    smite us.

History does not always tell the whole truth.

Destruction and the lapse into obscurity can come
    all too quickly, without horns trumpeting.

We will lose in the end. Have fun along the way.

Never pity yourself.

Touchstones and talismans give us some small
    measure of comfort.

424

40 Days, 40 Nights

{ 34 }

Some people will go to no end to preserve the mask.

*E*ven titans step into the twilight.

For whom the mad would destroy, first they make idols, gods and goddesses.

Ruthlessness, improvisation, dishonesty and old-world charm are attractive qualities in a person.

The stairway to excess is steep and shallow.

Always stare down mortality with defiance.

Sometimes sense, sensibility and shame must be abandoned.

Passion for what you do can sustain you.

An exquisite life encircles incredible highs, and terrible lows.

Both dark and light lead to oblivion.

The past can never be erased, merely covered up and left behind.

Rogues are never as dangerous as fools.

When the devil grew old he became a monk.

One's heaven is another's hell.

It is easy to get swallowed up in feeling, to
wallow in dark depths lost in a world of
sadness, anger, tears.

Let no man shackle your spirit.

There lives a hell box hole inside the head, the
center of all pain.

Internal demons are the most vicious, sneaky,
dangerous, destructive and seductive of all
known enemies and predators; and the most
elusive and difficult to destroy.

Many unseen images flicker in the dark.

We are enticed by that which causes trauma.

Pain is poetry of the mind.

Everything the power of the world does is done within a circle.

An unquiet mind is often disconnected and severed from the rest of the body, like a devil's head island, a haunted solitary place, of such incredible torment and torture, and also pleasure, onto itself.

Despite the darkness, there is ironic comedy.

Wanton wastrels make amusing party guests.

Too much wisdom is akin to foolishness.

A certain amount of madness can be quite fine, fun and intoxicating.

There is no such thing as the whole truth.

In life, find out what is true and what is meaningless and not worth pursuing.

Hatred is sometimes camouflaged with a smile.

Stranger, darker possibilities exist at every turn.

It is difficult and dangerous to be fully alive.

Death mingles among revelers.

Somewhere between reality and illusion, a thinly
disguised transparent screen shatters like a pane
of broken glass.

No one believes a liar when he tells the truth.

The sun rises on evil and good.

Each man rises highest when his path is unknown.

Disobedience reigns supreme.

Indispensable men wind up in the graveyard, just
like everyone else.

One devil does not make hell.

The judge of the law is always more powerful than
the law.

We create our own private, custom-tailored
 heavens and hells.

Look for the heart within the darkness.

Our deepest sorrows come from our greatest joys.

Serpents always lurk in paradise.

What keeps us going is a ridiculous mental tango
 with ourselves.

Drink and despair fuel creativity.

The portrait that we paint of ourselves is
 never accurate.

Unleash the inner wild that lives inside.

The sneakiest robbery is bloodless, with a
 fountain pen.

Life is a masquerade.

It is better to be a living dog than a dead lion.

It is better to look ill than old, as old age is
progressively terminal, with no cure.

Few people are half as good or bad as others
imagine them to be.

We focus on the lies as well as the truths.

Those who do nothing, say nothing, believe
nothing, and are nothing, are especially good at
avoiding criticism.

All triumphs come with a price, and a loss.

Poverty and wealth both fail to bring happiness.

We are all strangers in town.

Hypocrites, priests, thieves and kings all sup from
the same cup.

Torment feeds and fuels us.

Suffer fools gladly. After all, they could be right.

If not now, when?

We are all three people — as we see ourselves, as
    others see us, and as we truly are.

All life is littered with wreckage.

Conceit and arrogance are suits of armor for weak men.

Who knows what the ends of life are?

The delirium and dreamland of drink makes man
    forget for the moment that he, too, will one day die.

Rules rarely make sense.

Evil men would be far less treacherous and easier
    to spot if there was no good at all in them.

There is continuity amid chaos and confusion.

We are often liked more for our defects than for
    our good qualities.

You are your own spectral opponent.

A large ego and a small mind often come
    packaged together.

Being gracious is not always good.

Plotting revenge is generally more enjoyable in
    theory than in practice.

Do not drink liquor if you do not want to feel good.

We all carry pain in our heads.

Everyone needs illusion and self-deception.

Those who pray loudly and publicly often prey
    quietly and privately.

He who is anointed is usually a surprise.

Enjoy the plaudits before they turn into boos
    and hisses.

The illusion of power is powerful.

Worry changes nothing.

Season what you say with praise and flattery, and
   most will swallow it.

It does not matter to most people what you are,
   only what they think you are.

Troubled minds cause trouble for themselves.

Fame, fortune and poverty each acquaints a man
   with separate sets of strange bedfellows.

The quality of your life is the ultimate reality.

Death is what your whole life has been leading up to.

A backwards glance reveals much.

Many places must be left behind, whether you
   want to leave them or not.

The world is an ever-burning fire.

Creativity, like many things, cannot be learned.

One man's pain is another man's pleasure.

There is no need to be taught what is already inside.

Underneath the cloak of good, sometimes hides evil.

Those who duel with death, spit in his eye, and
     survive feeling fully alive.

Scoundrels make better dinner companions
     than martyrs.

Being uncomfortable makes us think.

In life we look for trapped-in-time places that
     make us feel part of the larger whole.

Unsaid sentiments become buried resentments.

We struggle to reconcile love and shame.

Pleasure seekers are envied.

We seek to see behind the barbed wire.

40 Days, 40 Nights

{ 35 }

*Secret places remind
us of who we are.*

$\mathcal{M}$any poison roots have a honeyed tip.

Dancing devils appear at dark, leading us to lonely
highways, the right road lost.

To wallow in the mire is good for the soul.

Find a tonic to transcend an ordinary world.

The absurd, impossible, unreasonable and
unexplainable intersect, lifting us to high places.

You have to believe in magic to see it, but not to
witness it.

All houses and fortresses are but sandcastles in
the surf.

Crumbling beauty cannot be denied.

The deepest, most damaging and deadliest betrayal is by
someone you thought you knew...loved...trusted....

Some wounds refuse to heal, ever.

Fools believe time is reality; time is an illusion.

The foundations of the earth are built and laid
upon the backs of nice people.

Mythical tragedies and fairytales are one.

Order emerges from chaos.

There is an active volcano inside, even though it
may appear dormant, and concealed.

A true happy ending is just a sleight of hand.

Death comes uninvited.

Shackles of the past forever bind tightly.

The veil of time and history often obscure heroes
and anti-heroes, as far as who is righteous and
who is wrong.

A touch of madness and magic are closely linked.

Everyone feels like he or she does not belong.

There are layers of unseen sludge and silt on every
soul, and psyche.

Everyone has something to despise, regret, desire.

Troubled minds should not always be pried open.

Paradigms and paragons are made to poke holes in.

Each moment is fleeting and irreplaceable.

The omniscient villain is never us, always
somebody else.

Good and evil are one.

What lies beneath the veil is not always a pretty sight.

The truth has a hard time being believed.

It is a long night's journey into the dim coldness of day.

The darkness brings power yet deception.

Suspicious minds plan the best offense.

Money and riches evoke passion. Murder. Insanity.
Intrigue. Envy. Betrayal.

There are many nightmares in dreamland.

Mortals love to drink from the poisoned chalice of
forbidden love.

A downward spiral can appear to be going in the
opposite direction.

Sometimes we harm ourselves to see if we can
still bleed.

The truth has an unwillingness to be seen.

You will have a long time to sleep when you are dead.

There is a season of discontent and malcontent.

We all get wounded along the way.

Treason and treachery come when least expected.

Suffering and survival walk hand-in-hand.

Time and tragedy sometimes bring about an
  unraveling and enlightening of the spirit.

Insurgents, anarchists and revolutionaries shape
  the world.

There is a bottomless black ocean inside.

Everyone cries secret tears that fill the urn of misery.

The stairwell to heaven passes through a descent
  to hell.

Miracles lie in the eyes and mind of the beholder.

Time runs backwards.

When we dream awake, the mind's eye is wide open.

The past cannot be undone.

From the darkness comes revelation and insight.

The cause of death is birth, so enjoy life.

It is the road that teaches us the best way to our destination.

The distinction between past, present and future is only an illusion, however persistent.

False friends make dangerous allies.

Humans are full of fragility, foibles and failure.

We either throw a romantic shroud over our past, or drown it in black ink.

Tear at the veil of pretensions.

Life is a looking glass of deceit and disillusion.

To travail the abyss, we must often take a quantum leap of blind faith.

Lingering shadows are the most dangerous.

Treachery and untruths are not visible to the naked eye.

All men have an abstruse appetite for bad.

Broken dreams and scars are the remnants of a
life lived.

The end of one era is the beginning of another.

We all live in prisons and castles of our own
making and design.

Forbidden things are always the most coveted.

Out of homage, comes self-salvation.

Man gathers strength and a sense of purpose from
myth, fairytales, fables and legends.

There is grave and casual chaos in life.

Neither dreamers nor doubters are immune to
knowing the wreckage of a crashed life.

The way you look should not be your identity.

Beauty queens never do feel beautiful, not really.

Everybody is born good, with the same size soul.

The end is the beginning.

While others hide behind lies, be a truthseeker
    and teller of the truth.

Brittle people usually break before they bend.

It is hard to leave the darkness for the light;
    brightness reveals our flaws and failures.

A map of menace and bones leads the way.

For that which is dead, birth is certain.

It is hard to escape the boundaries within our heads.

Dangerous liaisons are the most fulfilling.

The most precarious secrets are the ones we are
    afraid to tell ourselves.

Drunkenness reveals what soberness conceals.

The demon of fear that lives inside, keeping us locked in a hellish domain, is the hardest to conquer, vanquish and defang.

Revelry does not diminish remorse or regret.

There is a finite number of good tidings, countered by the bad ones.

It is frightening to do the arithmetic of time, and take measure of who you are.

The worst hells are private and unseen.

We all live on many levels.

Every tomb tells a tale and the whispers of the past lead the way to the future.

To know is not to know.

At the bottom of the abyss comes the voice of salvation, the black moment when the real message of transformation will be found.

We venture by night what we are afraid of by day.

Heroes and pariahs are interchangeable.

Life is a juxtaposition of violence and tenderness.

To stay alive, practice the fine art of magical thinking.

Life features recurring themes of refuge,
  displacement, and a yearning for beauty.

Woes of the world drench the sounds of sorrow.

The past is an unfaithful companion.

We love most what does not age in the memory.

Greed is comparative.

There is an underside to the floor you think you are
  standing on.

40 Days, 40 Nights

{ 36 }

Forbidden pleasures intoxicate us.

*A*ll life is a fight. Kick hard.

There is gravity with grace.

Ivory towers and gutters are not so very far apart.

Even gods and saints can be haunted, driven, pained,
  with a very dark soul and many demons inside.

The dream is often nothing but a nightmare.

Savage people often hide buried deep within the
  layers of sheep's skin.

Memory is but a metaphor.

A sense of menace is very appealing and seductive.

Today is a good day to evade tomorrow.

Sometimes it is best to forget and ignore what has
  been learned.

Life is a dazzling and deranged carnival.

There is a human impulse to rage, to rampage
and destroy.

Passion passes beyond good and evil.

There are many spiraling staircases that lead you
on a descent into darkness.

Silence is sometimes deafening.

The center is everywhere, the circumference
is nowhere.

Some things are perhaps worth giving up forever.

There is a time for adversity and for prosperity.

Life's path traces a contorted circle.

The riptides of life fluctuate back and forth,
sometimes sweeping in both directions at once.

What is lost seems more valuable.

The truth is rarely celebrated.

We are all grounded in false bottomless terrain,
    falling through the arc of darkness.

Time is forever running out.

Good always encounters resistance and obstacles.

Too much wisdom often leads to foolishness rather
    than good judgment.

We see what we want to see, not what is really there.

The world is filled with the darkness of light.

We live in a beautiful fragile world, that can be over
    in a moment.

Double-dealing is the rule of thumb.

People who always tell the truth are thought of as liars.

Cast off woulds, coulds, shoulds.

What we turn our backs on cannot always
    be reclaimed.

In people and in objects, time mars and scars
but it also adds a rich, age-worn patina of a
certain glow and luster that can neither be
rushed nor duplicated.

There are many fallen worlds.

Avoid staring at hearses; as they will be seeing you
soon enough.

High society leads people to low places.

Disharmony and discord create the friction that
keeps the world spinning on its axis.

Always be more than what people see.

It is difficult to stay on the path when you do not
know where or what the path is.

Upon the first whiff of weakness, or the proverbial
taste of blood, a man often becomes an animal
moving in for the kill.

Publicity, public relations and propaganda rule the
modern world.

He who helps everybody helps nobody.

The best advice and counsel comes from the
voice within.

A dark night has no witnesses.

It is not so unusual to live by clinging to the edge
of death.

Perfection is an insult to the gods.

The voice of reason and compromise is not always
the best voice to listen to.

Our lives are carved in sand.

There is a fascination for ruin that is romantic
and seductive.

No-fault misery is unavoidable.

Some people look the grim reaper in the eye and
like what they see.

Rip-current emotions prove we are alive.

We subsist in emptiness, exist in anguish and woe,
  but the sweet sorrow of love causes us to persist.

Some are able to travel beyond the boundaries that
  separate us.

Every moment is infinity.

Those who do not possess a great longing inside,
  achieve few things in life.

It is better to become a maverick first, and a
  martyr last.

Falsehood is common, truth uncommon.

The only way to never forget what you have
  learned, is to learn it the hard way.

Everybody's friend is nobody's friend.

Too much book sense can sometimes mean, and
  also lead to, no sense at all.

Pathbreakers possess the power to change the world.

Four eyes see more than two.

Many things are dim yet beautiful with eternal
twilight, and the passing of time.

Gloomy shadows often slumber in enchanted sunlight.

Scars on the skin and soul show you have lived.

Never is it born, never does it die.

Survival and power are commonly attained through
ruthlessness and betrayal.

Many ghosts of the past, shapes of pain and pleasure,
grow from the ground, crumbling from the walls,
stretching into the setting sun.

We live in the shadows of the veiled vale.

One man's punishment is another man's pearly gates.

The morbid can be humorous.

In the heat of the moment, false imagery can swarm
upon us.

There is no such thing as reality.

Many moments recede into the background, or move
forward, depending on how one prefers to see it.

There burns a bottomless cauldron deep inside of
everyone.

Every journey has a story.

The astute realize, and contemplate, we are all
strangers, voyaging in that strange land.

Close your eyes to see.

If you do nothing, you get criticized; if you do
something, you get condemned.

Mankind is always preoccupied with echoes.

Who does not wish to be a revolutionary, yet few
possess the courage and conviction.

Be not afflicted by the unavoidable.

Not everything needs to be acted upon.

Physical attributes should not be one's best attributes.

For every Eden there is a serpent.

Life is a three-ringed circus gone mad.

Savages should not be the only ones entitled to run
wild and free.

If your happiness is based on getting others' approval
on everything you do, you will fail, miserably.

Sometimes the veil is torn away, and you are seen
for what you are.

Not all predators are among the unwell.

Heaven can be found in the great emptiness of a
vast landscape.

One should wear their belongings lightly.

To disappear into a little twist of decadence is good.

Drama queens and drunks oftentimes rule the world.

Those who survive calamity, downfall and
destruction are reborn stronger.

A strange realm of otherwordly gossamer tenacious
magic is woven from the remnants of grief and loss.

Those who ask no questions lower their risk of
being told a lie.

It does not matter as much as you think it does.

We love an avenger.

There is a distant panorama of ghosts who speak in
the back of our heads.

Beware of deeds done in the name of a good cause.

It is not necessary to smile all the time.

40 Days, 40 Nights

❡ 37 ❡

*On that relentless march toward
the crypt, break rank, run away,
be as disobedient as possible.*

We seek to cure what we are inside.

There is always a trapdoor in the floor.

Provoke the world.

A festering abscess on the heart and soul is a
common affliction and impairment.

The windowpanes of hell are upon us.

In a moonlit nighttime sky, filled with stars, a
glimpse of the heavens can be seen.

Tears are souvenirs of things past, of loves lost.

Free-falling can take you down, or set you free.

Life is a windchime of haunting echoes.

There are nightmares to be found in the
American dream.

Burning down the road sets us free.

It is good to live on the fringes of society; the rules of normal society have no currency for those on the outer limits.

Many things are hauntingly familiar.

If you ignore it, the subconscious can reach up and grab you.

The dark angel of destruction sometimes brings light.

Conquest, conflict, controversy and curiosity change the world.

Rain evokes rainbows.

Many collision courses begin with a score to settle.

Who can define success, really?

The worst devils are the ones inside that fight us.

Leave room for mystery, the unknown, the transcendent and unexplainable.

An instant is an eternity. They are one.

Let go.

It is sometimes good to practice belligerence
    and debauchery.

With too much concentration on the flesh, the
    brain fades and withers.

Only rivers run free.

In the long run, the enviable are not always
    so enviable.

The shadow self always emerges, sooner or later.

Let intuition and gut instinct be your guide as to
    when to kick first.

The self cannot be slain.

Icons and exciting people eschew the trappings of
    normal society.

We implode and impale ourselves, with love and hate.

The stars are invisible to those who do not look skyward.

We fly away from ourselves to come back toward
the inside of who we really are.

Everything that is in your head and heart, you
carry with you, wherever you go.

Anguish and ecstasy are a revolving helm.

Possessions that you wear too heavily will eventually
crush and suffocate you.

In the revelation of what is perceived to be the
beginning and end, there is no alpha and omega,
only a delusion of such.

Might is above right.

All life is a puzzle of pitfalls, pleasures and peril,
pain and promise.

Romance is never third rate.

There is no guide to life; we wing it, dodging bullets
along the way.

When the cold winds blow in eight directions we
all need company.

Strange towns — people, places and things — can
seem familiar.

Life has the permanence and stability of sandcastles.

Destiny wears many drapings.

The unapologetically opinionated are often well
respected.

Spunk and sheer determination can triumph over
the worst of odds.

Tall shadows, darkly silhouetted upon the fluid
and ever-changing landscape, of the outer earth
and inner psyche, are never as big or fierce as
they look.

In a shimmering sense, life is illusory.

The closet is a suffocating place in which to live.

Internal earthquakes are the most jarring, alarming, and unsettling of all.

The best memoirs are the prickliest remembrances.

Passion is the quintessential essence of life.

Living with the actuality, and specter, of death alters the meaning of life.

Dare to be who you are.

There is no such thing as justice in the real world, so do not expect it.

We all play Chinese checkers with the game of Death and his partner, Life.

There are many cures available for pain and passion.

Swimming against the tide builds strength and character.

Thunderclouds bring more than rain, they bring
new life.

What is dormant can only remain hidden for so long.

Discontent is a disease with many faces.

Along the weirdly winding path of life, intrusions and
distractions are impossible to ignore or avoid.

Be sure you want to unveil the curtain that conceals.

We are all but blameless thieves and wretched
rainmakers who choose to sell, steal, barter and
ransom our souls, for something, or someone, at
one time or another.

Many things cannot be seen, until it is too late.

When the scalp prickles, beware.

The stars shall lead us to salvation, and oblivion.

It is easy to be blinded by rainbows and pots of gold.

Everything that has a beginning has an end.

All empires are transient and temporal, built on sand.

Man enjoys arguing with the handwriting on the wall.

All hail the hallowed halls of heaven and hell.

The eyes of evil are everywhere.

We all search for the secret place inside, where the
    seat of the soul resides.

The sanctity of life is transparent, opaque, murky
    and fleeting.

Many devils and devouring demons live deep
    within our heads.

Everything is always in flux.

There is a perilous and frayed line between reality
    and fiction.

Confessions should be raw and wildly personal.

A dark menace lurking just out of range, beyond
the corner of our eye, something we never really
quite see, drives us to great highs and despairs.

The prodigious pit of purgatory consumes us all.

Passionate outrage sometimes helps to fill a void in
the heart.

Those who enter into the vortex of the abyss
reemerge stronger, or else....

Life is a dubious illusion.

The highway to hell can lead to the promised land.

A poisonously destructive conscience, one that
thinks and feels and grieves too much, is the
worst kind of hell.

The lacquered trimmings of wealth are but
couturier armor.

Life is a carnival.

There is no real redemption, not really, only temporary refuge.

It is a harrowing journey for those who seek to capture and conquer the black heart of the American dream.

Dark clouds gather from the four corners of the world.

Life leaves a litany of loss but also a legacy of love.

Death marches through the wilderness, silently.

Who does not seek to touch that remembrance of things gone by?

Valiant deeds and treacherous ones are close.

When pushed to the edge, fight back, kick hard.

Survivors have a storied past.

We all slide down the slippery slope to our doom.

472

40 *Days,* 40 *Nights*

{ 38 }

Our garden of memories
is a place of reflections.

&xperience is a treacherous teacher.

A perilous line lives and lingers between success
   and disaster.

The material world feels good, for a while.

It is not always possible to hold the demons at bay.

What you fear will find you.

Missteps, slips and stumbles bring us down, yet
   redeem us as well.

What money cannot buy, the heart cannot erase.

Since balance holds dominion over all things,
   survival does not always go to the fittest or to
   the strongest, as many believe.

You can never be the person you used to be; the
   person you once were.

When masks are removed, illusions are shattered.

Pain is the seed of pleasure.

We are all dancing, running and crawling upon a
    terminally thin sliver of quickly melting ice.

The meaning of life and words changes with the
    passage of time.

Nothing remains forever.

You do not need to stray far to take a great journey.

Life requires a strong sense of humor and irony.

The world is best viewed through irreverent eyes.

Death is a participant in the bizarre party of life.

Those who dance are thought to be insane by
    those who do not hear the music.

We are all avengers of vice and masters of virtue.

There is an ominous cavern beneath the world we
    take for granted.

Fame and fortune are forged with a gilded cage.

Life is riddled with the abysses of human nature,
    cruelly lurking beneath the bland appearance
    of things.

Sometimes a surging sea can be poured from a teacup.

To fly to the highest point may require that you
    shut your eyes.

It is good to be feisty, self-reliant and rich.

The most important words in life are those written
    between the lines.

Insiders sometimes have no view of the outside.

Secrets are rarely secrets.

Fractured fairytales lure us in and take us down the
    rabbit hole.

Everything is transient.

To repair imperfect, slightly decayed beauty
sometimes destroys its essence, the thing that
makes it unique and attractive.

All things pretty often have a poisonous underbelly.

The river inside is a mosaic of mirrors.

It is impossible to outrun the inevitable. But it is
worth a try.

A ray of light always shines brightest when cloaked
in darkness.

To confront shadows is hard.

Life blooms wild for a season, surging forward like
the tide and then gradually slips back out; our
life leaves its mark for a while yet inevitably
another wave will wash over it and erase that
mark. The thing is, we hardly ever notice that
gradual recession. It is so quiet, so unassuming
that we never notice life is pulling away from us.

Make the iron hot by striking.

In the dark of night, all men are black.

Life is full of mystery, complication and upheaval.

Myth, mystery, magic and madness party together,
endlessly.

Great suffering is what makes the pleasures of life
so extraordinary.

Do not look into the mirror others hold up for you.

Pathos and tragedy spawn the seeds of comedy.

We are sucked toward a swirling black vortex.

Light penetrates dark; dark does not penetrate light.

We all play a losing game of hide-and-seek with a
shrouded invisible figure of death.

Life is a marvelous mystery that we will never get
to the bottom of.

Some horizons are vertical.

It is best to never reach the end of the rainbow.

Life is but a parody masquerade dance, a tango of
opposites, paired and reconciled as one.

It is sometimes good to keep yourself in the dark
as to the true nature of the world.

Many have faith in nothing.

There are unseen devils and demons everywhere.

Fear gives birth to many untruths.

The universe is an inherently balanced seesaw with
equal shares of good and evil, truth and lies,
strength and weakness.

Lawmakers are lawbreakers.

The permutations of a prince are rarely condemned.

In every person there exists both light and darkness,
good and bad.

Sanity and insanity are connected and separated by
a strand, a sliver.

Life is a paradox.

Nocturnal darkness comes as blessed relief from
the straitjacket of day.

Fashionable vices sometimes pass for virtues.

The gods, life and death are all masterly and
masquerading puppeteers.

It is taboo to bear the markings of an explorer or
outsider; these are the ones who live free,
though with great loneliness.

What is fleeting cannot be detained.

Only the brave and fearless dare to ask questions.

The pieces of the puzzle rarely fit together until it
is too late.

Prisons and paradises can become the same thing.

Following the path of most resistance brings the
    greatest fulfillment.

No one can outrun or beat time.

There lives a faint, quiet voice in the back of
    our minds.

Some things can never be changed.

Our most dangerous, destructive opponent hides
    in the shadows of our own mind, lurking in the
    dark recesses of our own selves.

Every revolution dies.

Blackness has a sneaky way of seeping into the chest.

Money is the root of all envy.

The curtain of chaos makes it difficult to see through
    the illusion of life.

Many things are possible by the light of the moon.

The truth does not always set you free.

In life, our paths intersect and diverge, and private
worlds collide, then move on.

There is always a price to pay for living in paradise.

Do not back down, even when standing poised at
the gates of hell.

It is okay to cry, and cry, aloud.

There are many who practice blatant soul-eating.

Many can never untie the gordian knot that binds
us to drowning.

Some trapeze, some traipse, through the twilight
of life.

Realness fades while impressions linger.

The self is the same forever.

We all walk alone, sooner or later.

It is better to stagger beneath a broken heart
   than to be afflicted with a hardened, hollow
   chest cavity.

People like gritty, idiosyncratic, mythologized
   places of ill repute that escape easy definition.

Some hungers are eternal.

The best things in life are humid, exotic, ungovernable.

Gloom and glitter rain down upon us.

When the muses sing, we cannot help but listen to
   the siren's song.

Our final vanquished secrets lie with the undertaker.

Be wary of affectionate contempt.

Life draws a delicate line between beauty and horror.

Sabotage is better than surrender.

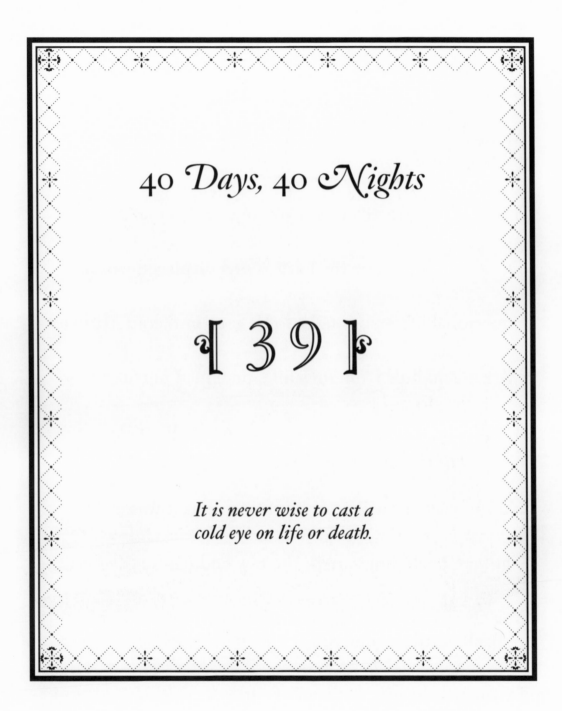

40 Days, 40 Nights

{ 39 }

It is never wise to cast a
cold eye on life or death.

*L*ife is full of echoes.

Who has not been stuck at the crossroads of an empty life?

There are no friends to get you out of this place.

Do not be beaten by the battles of a displaced world.

Traditional life maps ought to be torn into confetti.

We run and hide from invisible, imagined pursuers.

Those who run fast toward the flame are built for disruption.

Nothing can, or will, ever be the same as it was.

The ripe beginnings are in the raw endings.

You always have the ability and opportunity to fight back, until the day you are six feet under.

Instinct is the greatest tool of survival.

Sometimes it is good to live life as a fortress, fierce
and formidable.

It is hard to awaken from our slumber, for to be
fully awake is to see clearly.

Most humans are self-serving, immersed in their
own duplicity.

When the worlds move on, your illusions are gone.

Madness and death are life's constant companions.

Eternity is now.

Court clout, cachet, controversy and nonconformity.

Life is chaos revealed.

Even serpents hide behind the sun, moon and stars.

Life forever changes when a splinter of fear, riddled
with sudden knowledge of our own mortality, flies
across the room and lodges itself deep within us.

Survival is the only true measure of success.

Most people are driven by the dreams and demons
that haunt us.

Some things are beyond words.

The fetid, hot breath of an open grave is always
upon us.

We are all birds of passage, floating through
the twilight.

Fate deals many life-changing cards.

The place was always there waiting for us, but we
were not ready.

What is possible to believe is often only an illusion,
with a thinly-varnished veneer of chapter and verse.

Too much is never enough.

Our own holy grail, and pursuit of it, is what defines
us, and consumes us.

The sweetly strange and soothing slipknot of time strangles us, eventually.

We all walk and crawl upon the boulevard of broken dreams.

Being depressed, angry, bitter and miserable is far easier than being happy.

Truth resides at the end of a circle.

Beware of imposters at every turn, especially the one in the mirror.

What has been released from the genie bottle can never be reclaimed or recaptured.

Imitation kills individuality.

A brilliant mind is also tortured and conflicted.

The brevity of life is a pale shadow that haunts us.

Malcontents are driven to search for the noontime devil.

There are no random actions.

Amid the heart of utter desolation, lies a bittersweet
    sea of oblivion, a dark place that pulls us under
    where we drown in the abyss or rise again reborn.

There is no day without its nightfall.

Every day our life is irrevocably changed, forever.

The heart's wisdom has a more important message
    than anything else.

We die and resurrect ourselves many times in our life.

There is no dress rehearsal for life.

Often we can feel the cold paper-shellacked shell
    of our own ruined self.

Nobody ever finds happily ever after, not really.

We are intrigued by clandestine realms of the seedy,
    sinister, and sordid — lust, longing, violence, and
    ill-begotten wealth.

To be free, unchain your heart.

No color is deeper than that of a black heart.

The paradox of growth is: something is lost, but
   something is gained.

We are drifting down a river of fire that has no end.

The evocation of the past is a metaphor of the
   present, a warning and a promise.

At the darkest moment comes the revelation of
   light, we tell ourselves.

With each rising of the sun, a new chapter in your
   life has just begun.

It is impossible to avoid deception and disillusionment.

Unleash yourself.

We all carry around a terrible darkness, a mangled
   longing that lives deep inside.

Too much pride creates prejudice.

We all live inside such twisted cages, looking for a
    hero to set us free.

Things in life are never as vivid as they could be.

Fairytales are but a fraud, a cruel trapdoor that
    covers and conceals the netherworld.

A moment is a lifetime, a lifetime but a moment.

Nothing cannot exist forever.

Fear and self-loathing are common companions.

We are all lords and liars, masters and slaves.

Life is so cruel with its trickery; even those who know
    great happiness and love are left with nothing.

We all do a delicate waltz with denial and destiny.

Do not be afraid to cradle convictions close to
    the chest.

Intense power and pathos are linked.

Wistful pacts with fate are designed to be betrayed.

There is no such thing as the real world.

Dwelling on the past is not useless, as answers unfold
from the past and the new day.

Seeking to avoid being pulled down by the silent
undertow, we distance ourselves from dark waters.

Life gives, life takes.

Reminders of mortality cannot be erased but are
fixed in time and our own psyche.

Nothing is greater than the force of the human soul.

Sometimes solitude helps us to collect the errant
parts of ourselves that have wandered away, and
to reassemble them.

All things are temporal and fleeting.

The pall of melancholy covers us, suffocating us.

We move intrepidly foward, reaching back to
    capture scenes from our past.

Those who look too deeply in the mirror often see
    a monster.

What breaks the heart can buttress the soul.

The scenery is often pretty while the street signs
    direct us along the road to nowhere.

We all fall through a crack in the edge of the
    world, eventually.

Catastrophe reins over beauty, and you need one to
    have the other.

We are never severed from the pieces of the past
    because history chases us.

Time seems to float gently like a butterfly, but that
    is deceit; for time marches upon us unheeded
    and unbridled, relentlessly, trampling all with no
    regard for anyone.

Who has not sung sorrow, romanticized misery?

Sweetly written memoirs of fate are seldom truthful.

We all love what is flawed, illogical and irrational.

Good intentions melt away like mist in the
morning sun.

The slide into personal madness is not always easy
to postpone.

Decrepit phantoms of yesterday sit perched on the
window sill, staring back at us.

Tortured lives hide behind shenanigans.

We wrestle with what we embrace.

In life, one picks either the rollercoaster or the
merry-go-round; then you ride out your choice.

Childhood memories live in haunted houses.

40 Days, 40 Nights

[40]

We walk away from our old ways but they return to torment and haunt us.

$\mathcal{M}$avericks must accept that they risk ridicule.

Live the day with intemperance; fight the break of
   dawn, delay the misery of tomorrow.

The odds are always daunting. Expect it.

Some feel immune from the truth and safe from
   the brink, but they, too, will learn that there is
   no escape.

Dancing is close to flying, unfettered.

No one knows exactly how far away are heaven
   and hell.

Be unpredictable and presume nothing.

Nothing obliterates the past; we have to confront
   it, one way or another.

Pallbearers are the pillars of the world.

We struggle against bitterness and gloom.

It is comforting to salute the soliloquies and epithets
     of yesterday; the memoirs and reflections of what
     was, and what is, our past.

Lovable rogues lead the way to hazard and
     Heartbreak Hotel.

There is no gatekeeper of the true truth.

Some can stand in the tide and virtually ignore it.

We often forge our own undoing.

The lords that rule over the ruins of lost kingdoms
     are never far from hand.

Strange fruits blossom from poisoned soil.

Most like the feeling of being another person; for a
     day, for a moment, forever.

We fuel our fears and feed our fantasies.

Those born with a silver spoon in their mouth
     often swallow it.

Incandescent rage lights up life.

Most come to accept that shifting lives are trapped in
    a rotating pendulum of holy and unholy ruin and
    recovery, of heartbreak and joy, of despair and bliss,
    of anguish and euphoria. This rite of passage, of
    destiny, cannot be denied.

Passion and commitment will keep you young.

There are many secrets outsiders are not permitted
    to observe.

Dreams often lead to schemes.

We ordain the parameters of our stalking shadows.

At dusk, the night is golden with promise.

It is okay to violate and bend the so-called rules of
    normal protocol, as not all subscribe to the norm.

Guilt and gilt come between people.

We see others through a glass window.

Unconventional people encounter out-of-the-ordinary
   amorous seductions, mistaken identities, festive
   nuptials, elegant parties, graveyard encounters.

Forbidden pleasures intoxicate us.

A twist of decadence and depravity is known to many.

Dark labryinths are endless and engrossing.

Many are plagued and bewildered by the persistent,
   nagging feeling that we are in the wrong life.

The world promises distress and uncertainty.

We ought to live in a world where magic is possible.

Try to ignore the fragility of luck.

Fear, loathing and loneliness wither the heart,
   turning us into brittle antique dolls.

Sunbeams do not compensate for darkness.

Memory reclaims what is lost but still present.

Many find fabled beauty and invigoration in the ugliness of things broken, more so than in the treacherous perfectionism of false fronts and perfumed boudoirs.

Sometimes there is nowhere left to run.

Heroes in death were not always heroes in life.

Secret places remind us of who we are.

It is good to toast and mock ourselves with great gusto and satire, mimicking our many shortcomings and foibles.

Repent tomorrow, but postpone tomorrow.

The raw condition of being human is to be flawed, vunerable, fragile and allowed to fail, yet able to then pick ourselves up and try again.

Never believe your own bravado and tall tales.

Those who choose to listen to their inner consciousness must summon much strength and determination.

Icons become casualties.

Many things spark a memory of moments we have
    never known.

Tattered, scattered lives are seductive.

Divine interception and inspiration can only be
    understood and confirmed by the believer.

Predators are often pretty.

A bottomless loneliness hides just behind the eyes.

Life is a series of chapters, a continuum.

The street, a place of real people, is the best place
    to find icons, stimulation, and inspiration.

We recreate a world that never was.

Those who have known the nose-pressed-against-
    the-window feeling of not belonging always
    carry that feeling.

Conceal your shadow.

We rarely walk away from the rapture of wicked ways.

Snap judgments are most reliable.

We cast a calloused eye on cautionary tales.

Illicit and thwarted passion either kills us or haunts
    our waking moments and sleepless nights.

What appears to be broken might not be.

The downfall of hard times leads to murk and morass,
    and perhaps the muddled road to redemption.

Rely on the unknown.

If you feel you have something to say, say it.

Who or what we are under the influence of, that is
    what molds us.

Go with the gut.

Uncivilized moments are the most memorable.

We are never out of the woods.

Memory is a loutish place of mistaken moments
and identities.

The past seems like somebody else's life.

Ruthlessly manicured hedges surround the rich.

Mischief is the best weapon of choice.

The unforgivable is unforgettable.

We lament the loss of those who have become floating
strangers to us, and sense only those empty places
of our past that we no longer recognize.

Be impetuous.

We are never smarter than the darkly-encased
inner miseries that encumber us.

Transgressions help us escape.

Even citadels corrode and crumble.

Most who change the course of history have an
    edge that breaks with the trappings of what
    came before.

The future is uncertain, the past familiar.

Beyond the darkness and the damage, the existentialist
    despair, there is defiance, and reinvention.

That which snares us behind the eyes, in the head,
    and undeneath the skin, sways and consumes us.

What is raw, hilarious and unsettling is also
    very attractive.

The charm of a rebel surpasses that of a saint.

When golden treachery runs rampant, truth and
    fiction are indistinguishable.

It is possible to be merry in misery.

Secret places remind us of who we are.

Cold people stand stoic as a petrified forest.

Dark, painful places decay us, but we step through it.

Celebrate rather than surrender.

We admire outlaw people who say and do what
    they want; what we are too polite or repressed
    to express.

Those touched by the fire are lovers of unreason.

We pace in our towers; a part of us waiting for life
    to begin.

Life seldom proceeds in an orderly sequence.

We cannot be protected from pain.

The raven waits for us.

Eat, drink and be merry, for then you think you
    will never die.

Postscript: Our Defining Moment

Grappling through writing with the dark shadows of loss, uncertainty and self-torment — to know you made a mark — helps to tame the pain. Commemoration and valiant hearts transform the face of tragedy. Once someone survives catastrophe the future looks different; suffering takes on a different meaning, and laughter, too. As I have heard and now believe, if you bring forth what is inside you it will save you; if you do not it will destroy you. Our city creates and memorializes something tangible and intangible, something poignant; it makes us feel less consumed and devoured by remembrances of disaster.

We often think our pain separates and alienates us, but actually it unites us in a profound manner. It is shocking, humbling and eye opening to face the panoramic picture of how isolated we sometimes think we are when swimming in a pool of pain, suffocating in the hurts of tragedy and trauma. Although others rarely experience our particular devastation, expressive storytelling appeals to and links the human spirit in a special way. We feel alone in our own vale of tears and in our individual pond of pandemonium when actually it is a vast global ocean, a universal waterway that connects and enlightens. To recall our own private purgatories and personal nightmares, we are able to transcend the moment.

As we learned with Katrina, and as others learn with their own adversities, we are capable of more than we learned or imagined. I think all post-disaster writing takes on a deeper, more esoteric meaning and significance with an urgency to seek truths and search out answers even when they might not exist. We see beyond our fond illusions and delusions. There is no painless passage. I notice that after Katrina I call upon ecclesiastic words and imagery far more often than in the past, in a way that still baffles me; it flows straight through me from a deep and mysterious well inside. Disaster bares us, strips us of our veils and yet, curiously, empowers us.

The clock and the church bells toll, and the band and the music play on. We know we will lose in the end but we intend to have fun along the way. New Orleanians accept that the edge of the abyss is always nearby and unpredictable, and that is what attracts us to angels in the mud and cherubs in the window.

Author Lagniappe

TJ Fisher (tjfisher.com) is the award-winning author of *Orléans Embrace*, an emotional portrayal of the unforgettable people and places of New Orleans. The post-Katrina work won the prestigious PMA Benjamin Franklin 2007 gold medal for "Best New Voice Nonfiction."

Known as an idiosyncratic writer of potent and poetic prose, flamboyant French Quarterite Fisher is a colorful character with a distinctive New Orleanian psyche. A consummate storyteller and chronicler of life, a lover of legacies who celebrates triumph over sorrow, she drives a 1959 pink Caddy convertible. Drawn to chase and challenge the dark crevices, melodramas and riddles of life, Fisher's nonfiction and fiction writings center on New Orleans. The media call her diverse works "engaging ... enchanting ... evocative."

Fisher is a longtime member of the Writers Guild of America, Directors Guild of America, Producers Guild of America, Dramatists Guild, Academy of Television and Arts and Sciences, Screen Actors Guild and Actors' Equity Association, and other professional guilds and organizations.